PICTORIAL HISTORY
of
AYR

Dane Love

COVER:
Oil Painting by Hugh Rankin
The Brigs of Ayr

© Dane Love 1995

First Published in 1995
by Alloway Publishing Ltd.,
Darvel, Ayrshire.

Printed in Scotland
by Walker & Connell Ltd.,
Hastings Square,
Darvel, Ayrshire.

ISBN No. 0-907526-58-6.

PICTORIAL HISTORY
of
AYR

Dane Love

Alloway Publishing

Auld Ayr, wham ne'er a town surpasses,
For honest men and bonie lassies

R. Burns

HISTORICAL SKETCH

Ayr is a very ancient town, standing at the mouth of the river of the same name. Where the name came from no-one knows, but it is believed to be an extremely early name, given at first to the river, and has the same root as the River Aire in Yorkshire, perhaps meaning "strong river". Today the town extends south over the River Doon, encompassing the village of Alloway, and north to Prestwick, a burgh founded around 1170.

The first settlers at the mouth of the Ayr were probably the Mesolithic hunters, who travelled around the country gathering food and hunting animals. Remains from this period have been found within the town and in the adjacent parish. At the end of Stonefield Avenue in Doonfoot is a standing stone which it is believed dates from the Neolithic period and may have been upended by Stone-Age man as a place of sun worship. Further evidence of Stone-age man include two stone axeheads which have been unearthed at Doonfoot.

The Bronze Age people left more relics, burial urns and cairns being discovered at Cambusdoon, Alloway and Doonfoot. Also in the Alloway area was the Bronze Age cairn after which Cairn Crescent was named, and which was mentioned in "Tam o Shanter" as the place "Whare hunters fand the murder'd bairn". The cairn was excavated in March 1963 prior to being destroyed when the ground was developed for housing. It was found to contain no relics of burial, but on the periphery a cist was later found, containing burnt bones.

Following the arrival of Christianity to Scotland in the 4th century, missionaries quickly arrived in the Ayr area. At Cambusdoon they erected a stone cross-slab, on which was carved a simple cross made up of inscribed arcs. This was discovered in 1928 by a pupil of Cambusdoon School and is now located in Loudoun Hall.

At Alloway a motte was constructed in the last few decades of the 12th century as the seat of a feudal baron. However, it is thought that this was abandoned soon after, when Ayr Castle was erected.

In 1197 King William the Lion ordered a new castle to be built between the Doon and Ayr. Historians have disagreed where this castle was located, but old maps indicate that a low mound in the back garden of 8 Montgomerie Terrace was where it stood. A document of the time records "William, Sheriff of the new castle on the Ayr". It is believed the castle was a wooden structure and that the castle shown on the burgh arms is quite an accurate representation of the building — a great octagonal tower to which is connected barmkin walls with two lesser towers.

William the Lion created the Royal Burgh of Ayr on 21st May 1205. The community was located on the south side of the river for a simple reason — the north side was in FitzAlan hands and they, not the king, would have gained the profits. The lands of Newton passed into Stewart hands, and they were granted the burgh charter of Newton-upon-Ayr sometime between 1314 and 1371. Newton never did rival the royal burgh, eventually being absorbed by the greater burgh in 1873. That Newton is an old foundation itself, predating the Auld Brig, is indicated by the fact that Main Street is aligned on the New Bridge, site of the ancient ford across the river.

The new burgh had the right to hold markets and fairs and because of its royal foundation also had the privilege of trading with foreign ports. The burgh at that time comprised of only one street (now called the Sandgate) and the ancient Church of St John. Within ten or twenty years of being raised to a Royal Burgh the community had extended upstream on the south side of the river to create what is now the High Street, as far as Carrick Street and Mill Street, where "ports" or gateways protected the town.

The site of most of these ports have been marked by plaques on the walls of adjacent buildings. They were Kyle Port in the High Street, replaced later by the Over Port in Kyle Street and Cow Port in Alloway Street when the town expanded, the Auld Tour Port in Mill Street, the Sandgate Port, and Brig Port on the Auld Brig.

New feus were laid out along the High Street, and the king bestowed certain privileges on those who took up these lands. He gifted 2,300 acres of ground to the burgh, known as the Burrowfield, from "burgh fields", which was divided into six acre plots for each burgher. The town grew quickly, becoming the main seaport along this coast, a prominent market town and centre of legal administration for the Sheriffdom of Ayr, which covered Carrick, Kyle and Cunninghame, later known as Ayrshire.

A charter of 1236 issued by King Alexander II gifted the fishing rights of the rivers Ayr and Doon to the burgh in order to pay for the upkeep of the harbour and the bridge. Some accounts say this bridge, originally timber in construction, was replaced by a stone structure that year, though other accounts place its year of construction as 1491. At the same time the burgh acquired the lands of Alloway, Corton and Carcluie. From these lands the burgesses could take timber for the building of houses and ships. In 1261 the king granted

Ayr with the right to hold a fifteen day long fair to be held in midsummer following the Feast of the Nativity of St John the Baptist.

The town suffered attack by Norwegian forces in 1263. King Haco IV of Norway planned to take the castle and town and subsequently the west of Scotland. Knowing of the proposed attack, the great western tower of St John's Church was erected to block what had previously been a glazed window. For three weeks twenty men were hired by the sheriff of the town to guard the castle. However, a storm in the Firth of Clyde wrecked a number of the Viking longboats and the remainder were soundly defeated at the Battle of Largs.

Just over thirty years later, in 1296, an English army invaded the town. They took over the castle and used the Barns of Ayr as a garrison for their troops. In 1297 William Wallace, the great freedom fighter, came to Ayr and set the

The Wallace Monument on Barnweill Hill

barns alight. Although it has been claimed that he killed hundreds of English troops by fire, this has been disproved; instead he burned the barns to prevent them being used by the foe. Wallace travelled to Barnweill Hill from where he watched the flames, and a great monumental tower was erected there in 1855 to commemorate this. In 1898 this tower was passed into the ownership of the Burgh of Ayr. The Barns of Ayr stood at what is now the south-eastern end of Mill Wynd, behind the High Street.

Robert the Bruce, son of the Earl of Carrick and probably born at Turnberry Castle, came to the town in 1298 and set the castle, still held by the English, on fire. However, it was repaired soon after and remained in foreign control. William Wallace was captured at Robroyston near Bishopbriggs and tradition asserts that he was held for a time in Ayr Tolbooth

prior to his transportation to London and decapitation. For this reason a statue of the great patriot was erected on the old tolbooth building in 1810 and later re-located on the present building (75 High Street) which was erected in 1886 to the plans of Allan Stevenson.

Robert the Bruce carried on his fight for independence, gradually gaining the upper hand, winning at Loudoun Hill in 1307 and ordering the destruction of Ayr Castle in 1312 to prevent it passing into enemy hands once again. Following his victory at Bannockburn in 1314, he came to Ayr on 26th April 1315 and held a meeting of Parliament in St John's Church at which the royal succession was settled. In 1315 Edward Bruce, his younger brother, left Ayr harbour to invade Ireland where he was crowned king in 1316. For their part in the battle at Bannockburn, forty eight men of Newton were granted Royal Freedoms, with Freedom Lands surrounding the burgh. These survived until the 19th century.

In the latter half of the 14th century sand blown from the shore threatened the church and town. A number of proposals were made to try and solve this problem, such as granting the lands to those who could reclaim it. In 1425 the Sandgate was narrowed in a further attempt at a solution, but until the citadel walls were built, thus sheltering the town, the problem did not go away.

By the 16th century Ayr was the leading port in the west of Scotland, with ships trading as far afield as Ireland and France. Woollens, skins, leather and cured fish were exported; iron, salt, flour and wine being brought in.

The lands of Alloway had been created into a parish of its own, the old church having been erected sometime around the end of the 13th century and traditionally dedicated to St Mungo. The church may have been extended or rebuilt in 1516, which date appears on a lintel. The bell, which is still in the belfry, is inscribed "FOR THE KIRK OF ALOUAY 1657".

The plague struck Ayr in 1545 and recurred for a century thereafter. To prevent travellers entering the town and passing on the Black Death the ports were guarded all night long and various back vennels were stopped up. Those affected were isolated on the burgh moor and should they try to re-enter the town they were subject to death by hanging.

Mary Queen of Scots visited Ayr in 1552 and again in 1563. On the second visit she had "soupper et coucher at St Jehan d'Era".

The High Tolbooth in the Sandgate was erected in 1575, replacing the Laigh Tolbooth which had been located in the High Street. To this tower, which had a courthouse and gaol attached, a belfry was added in 1615, the bell cast in Irvine and the clock made in the town by John Smyth. The Laigh Tolbooth was demolished in 1826, the stone being bought by John Robb of Blackburn who used it to construct a wall round his property. Three stones in this wall, in front of the Gartferry Hotel in Racecourse Road, are still pointed out as being the very stones to which the burgh gibbet was affixed.

In 1563 the Scots parliament pronounced witchcraft to be a capital offence and the first local victim, the Witch of Barnweill, was burned in 1586. The most famous Ayr witch was Maggie Osborne, who kept an inn at 78 High Street. She was blamed for many misdeeds and was executed and buried in the yard of St John's Tower. Bessie MacCallan was imprisoned in 1650 under suspicion of witchcraft and was probably hanged, making her the last local person to suffer this fate.

By the middle of the 17th century Ayr had grown to a town of around two thousand inhabitants. It was still an important seaport, exporting woollens, leather, plaid, fish, salt and coal, while from places like France, Netherlands,

Ayr at the beginning of the seventeenth century

Norway and the Baltic wine, cloth, spices, fruit, wax, timber, iron, canvas, tar and cattle were imported. Twenty large ships worked from the harbour, but trade diminished with the arrival of the Cromwellian troops. In 1656 it was noted that there were only three ships trading from the harbour plus two small barques carrying coal. The trade had mainly transferred to the growing city of Glasgow. In 1670 the town council noted that "Our harbour is totally ruined and decayed quhilk we are not abill in the least to maintain. Our bridge daylie failing by great spaits, and yce coming down in the winter tyme on it."

Between 1652 and 1654 the soldiers under Oliver Cromwell arrived in Ayr and took over St John's Tower. Around it, and using stones brought from Ardrossan Castle, they constructed a vast fort, extending to 12 acres, which was basically hexagonal in plan but which had projecting corners. The walls were made of earth piled up, the exterior revetted with stonework. A moat was dug on the landward side of the walls, and a single entrance passed through the walls. The plans for the fort were designed by Hans Ewald Tessin, Cromwell's engineer.

The fort was designed to accommodate hundreds of soldiers, and the kirk tower was used as a lookout post. The fort remained garrisoned until 1660, the year the Protectorate ended and Charles II was restored to the throne.

The lands occupied by the fort were in 1663 granted to the Earl of Eglinton as a Burgh of Regality, called Montgomerieston. The earl had great plans for the community and initially the Royal Burgh was afraid of the possible loss of trade which this may have caused, but Montgomerieston did not prosper and was eventually absorbed into Ayr.

In January 1691 the parish of Alloway was annexed to that of Ayr. The folk of Alloway fought against this, sending petitions to Edinburgh, but the Magistrates of Ayr felt that the merging would be "of great advantage both to the Burgh and barony." The ministers of Ayr held irregular services in the church of Alloway, and it was for a time used as a schoolroom. Around the year 1760 the church was abandoned,

and the roof subsequently fell in.

At the end of the 17th century Ayr was very much a town in decline and various accounts by visitors of the time make sorry reading. One of the later visitors, Daniel Defoe, wrote:

> *The capital of this country is Air, a sea-port, and as they tell us, was formerly a large city, had a good harbour, and a great trade: I must acknowledge to you, that though I believe it never was a city, yet it has certainly been a good town, and much bigger than it is now. At present like an old beauty, it shows the ruins of a good face; but is also apparently not only decayed and declined, but decaying and declining every day, and from being the fifth town in Scotland, as the townsmen say, is now like a place forsaken; the reason of its decay, is, the decay of its trade.*

EIGHTEENTH CENTURY

The Union of Parliaments in 1707 resulted in an increase in trade in Ayr and the town began to thrive again. The harbour was improved — a small lighthouse was put up in 1712 and the quay improved the following year. In 1724 the Convention of Royal Burghs granted the town £40 towards the repair of the harbour. More improvements were made to the quays and dredging of the river bed commenced in 1730.

The Over or High Tolbooth in the Sandgate was in need of repair and in 1726, when the old Church of St John was being demolished, stone was taken for this purpose. A new steeple was added, complete with bell and clock. The building was restored again in 1754 and although in 1785 Robert Adam provided a set of plans for the rebuilding of the Tolbooth these were not used.

The Burgh of Ayr installed street lighting in 1747, but only in the town centre. A burgh slaughterhouse was also established, in Mill Vennel, where there was also a brewery and tanning workshop. In 1749 William Duff applied to build a linen factory in the same street but despite this introduction of a form of mass production, Duff's spinning works did not succeed.

The grounds of Alloway were sold off in a roup in 1754, raising £7,190 Sterling which was used to help pay off the burgh's public debts. Extending to 2,335 acres, the lands were divided into 28 parcels. Each extent of ground was generally bought by those landowners in the town who wished to get out into the country. Rozelle and Belleisle estates were established at this time, Rozelle having been bought by Robert Hamilton who had returned from Jamaica and named his new grounds after a plantation which he owned. Other estates which developed from this time include Mountcharles, Greenfield, Gearholm and Doonholm.

In 1758 a poors house was erected in Mill Vennel by the burgh, funded from the Alloway sale. This continued in use until 1860 when the Kyle Union Poorshouse in Holmston Road was opened. The old poors house was converted to an abattoir which remained until the present Mill Street sheltered houses were erected on the site, a new slaughter house being erected at Heathfield.

The community of Wallacetown was established in 1760 by the Wallaces of Craigie House. They laid out a number of feus on King (originally Cross) and Wallace streets. The Gordons of Blackhouse laid out a regular grid of feus adjoining Wallacetown which was known as Content, comprising John, Content, James, Elba and Church streets. Content became regarded as part of Wallacetown, the Wallacetown Parish Church being erected there in 1834. The community was popular with workmen as it was located outwith the Royal Burgh and was therefore not subject to the same tight restrictions laid down by the various trade guilds.

The 18th century also saw improvements in transport. In 1777 the gateway and gatehouse at the north end of the Auld Brig were demolished, the ruins of which were incorporated in later buildings. It is the ruins of these later buildings which can be seen today. The other ports at the end of the Sandgate and High Street were also removed, allowing easier access for horse-drawn carts.

Around the year 1767 the street now known as Newmarket Street was laid out. Previously there had been a tree-lined close between the back rigs of the houses, as shown on early maps, but it was opened up as a proper street and used to give access to the new Butter Market, hence its name.

Even more significant was the erection of a new bridge across the river. The Auld Brig was rather narrow and steep for modern carriages and so in 1785 the burgh received an Act of Parliament allowing them to construct a New Bridge. This was located downstream from the Auld Brig, at a spot originally used as a fording point. A few buildings at the end of the Sandgate had to be demolished to allow the new access road (New Bridge Street) to pass through. On the north side of the river the bridge arrived at the spot where previously Newton Mill had stood.

The original plans for the New Bridge were designed by Robert Adam. This was a very grand classical structure, with balustrades, statues and carved stones. The cost of this was £4000, to be recouped from tolls paid on crossing. However, a simpler version was built, still quite a fine structure, but one which turned out to be weak. Alexander Stevens, a local architect, may have been responsible — he erected a fine double bow-fronted house for himself at the southern end, still seen when crossing the present bridge. Local masons constructed the bridge between 1785-88, but Burns' prophecy in "The Brigs of Ayr" that the Auld Brig would outlast the New came true when in 1877 a severe series of floods destroyed the New Bridge. A second New Bridge was subsequently built at the same spot.

Around the year 1800 the old moat of the fort was filled in and Academy Street (later renamed Fort Street) constructed along the back of the Sandgate gardens. This prompted development in this area, a new church and school being erected there.

NINETEENTH CENTURY

The beginning of the 19th century was one of great prosperity in the burgh and the population of the town passed the 5000 mark. It was at this time the formal terraces around Wellington Square area were erected, and the better off residents moved into them, leaving behind the old and overcrowded houses in the town centre. Many of the buildings in the Wellington Square vicinity were town houses used by the landed gentry of the county, replacing the older buildings which they owned in and around the High Street or Sandgate. The use of town houses died out during the 19th century, but a few existed into the 20th century with

one of the last to be sold being No. 1 Wellington Square, town house of Mrs Hay-Boyd of Symington, which she retained into the 1920s. When she arrived in the burgh in her carriage and pair it was described as a "notable sight".

The first new terrace was constructed in Barns Street, the north side of that new roadway being erected about 1815. Previously the roadway from Carrick Vennel (or Street as it is now) carried on in a straight line past Barns House to join what is now Racecourse Road at the south end of Barns Terrace. On the south side of Barns Road Berkeley House was erected in 1803, and across the street on the south side of what became Wellington Square, Wellington House was erected in 1806 by Provost Charles Shaw, though it did not bear this name until 1815, when the victory at Waterloo was orchestrated by the Duke of Wellington.

South of Wellington Square there was to be a second square, known as Alloway Square after David Cathcart, Lord Alloway, who owned the lands on which it was to be built. The proposed square is shown on Wood's map of the town published in 1818 but only the terraced houses in Alloway Place were built, Park Terrace being built at a later date. (The architect John Robertson prepared plans for this square, which would have measured 240 feet by 172 feet).

Charlotte Street, running parallel with Wellington Square, was created around 1810. Miller Road (or Place as it was originally named, after Provost Hugh Miller) was laid off as a turnpike road in 1846 but the houses were not erected along its length until the 1850s or 1860s.

In Newton-upon-Ayr (around the year 1820) Green Street and York Street were laid out in a grid pattern. Each of these streets had a back lane, and transverse streets were created at Clunes Vennal and Halls Vennal/Taylor Street.

Shop in Hope Street being re-thatched

The remaining lands of Newton were feued from around 1834 onwards and the final lands were built on in the 1880s. A number of large houses were erected here in a similar manner to the First Ward, but over the years these have been replaced and the area fails to have so "rich" a feel as the south side of the town. Of these large houses Woodfield (circa 1833) survives as Dalblair Motors, Falkland is "lost" in Falkland Place and Newton Lodge was demolished.

The early years of the 19th century were noted as a time of worry, for body snatching was rife. Bodies were dug up from fresh graves and transported to the universities of Glasgow or Edinburgh for dissection. To prevent this from happening various deterrents were used, from having a constant watch in the kirkyards, to the affixing of a "mortsafe" over the coffin for a number of weeks, until the corpse was too decayed to be of any use. Two mortsafes, one dated 1816, hang in the Auld Kirk's lychgate and others are in Kirk Alloway. It is known that a number of corpses were stolen, however, for in 1831 empty coffins were discovered at Newton.

In 1825 the council decided to erect a new town hall and burgh chambers. The architect Thomas Hamilton of Edinburgh was engaged and he produced a classical edifice which was very much in vogue at the time. Incorporating a magnificent 225 feet tall spire, the buildings were erected in the Sandgate, facing the old tolbooth.

As well as much new building in the town, there was a considerable amount of demolition going on. The burgh council had decided on a policy of improvement, and began clearing away a number of old buildings, either rebuilding them or leaving the site bare in order to create space. Buildings which were cleared away included the Laigh Tolbooth (1810), Fish Cross, High Tolbooth (1826) and the Auld Wallace Tower.

At the beginning of the 19th century dissent began to grow over the right to vote. In 1819 a meeting of "Reformers" took place in the town, and John Taylor campaigned for the widening of the franchise. At the first election following the introduction of reform which was held in December 1832, Taylorists rioted in the town. However, T.F. Kennedy was voted in as the Whig M.P. for Ayr Burghs, Taylor coming second, and the Tory third.

At the time of reform the communities of Newton-upon-Ayr, Wallacetown and Content were linked with Ayr as a parliamentary constituency. There were also proposals to create a greater burgh of Ayr incorporating these communities, but the people of Ayr felt that they would be liable for supporting the poor of Newton, and the folk north of the river did not wish to be liable for the Royal Burgh's debts. The communities were therefore linked until 1873 when the Burgh of Ayr Act was ratified in parliament.

The prosperity of the town was shown by the foundation of a new newspaper. The "Air Advertiser" first appeared on 5th August 1803, covering not only the county but also much of south west Scotland, for which Ayr was something of a market and provincial centre. The "Ayrshire Post" first appeared in 1880. Other newspapers included the "Ayr Observer" (1832-1930), "Ayr and Wigtownshire Courier" (1818-25) and the more recent free papers such as the "Ayrshire World" and the "Ayrshire Leader".

Burns' Monument at Alloway

A gasworks was built outwith the western wall of the fort in 1826, operated by the British Gas Company. The folk of Newton built their own gasworks in 1845, located off Weaver Street. The gas companies were nationalised in 1949 but following connection to the North Sea gas-fields the works were closed down and cleared away.

In 1840 a gravitational feed water supply was laid into the town from the Milton Springs on Carrick Hill. A number of fountains were subsequently presented to the town, including the Steven Fountain off Bath Place in 1892 and the fountain in Burns Statue Square presented by William MacKerrell in 1868. New reservoirs were opened by 1870 but the supply could not cope with the demand. The water-supply was taken into burgh care in 1873 and in 1887 Loch Finlas in Straiton parish, eighteen miles distant from the town, was dammed and a pipe laid to channel the waters to the ever-thirsty residents. As part of the scheme filter beds were constructed at Knockjarder near Dalrymple.

Things improved greatly with the arrival of the railway in 1839. The line extended south from Glasgow through Paisley and Irvine to a terminus at North Harbour Street and there were great celebrations when the first engine chugged its way into the station on the 5th of August. The link north through Beith to Glasgow was opened in August 1840 thus connecting Ayr by rail to the rest of Britain. The folk of Glasgow discovered the beaches of Ayrshire were within a reasonable distance and soon day-trippers and holidaymakers flocked to the coast.

In 1857 the line was built south to Dalmellington, in order to export iron from Waterside. From Falkland Junction a new line was laid to the east of Wallacetown to a new railway bridge across the river. A new station, originally known as Townhead Station, was erected at the top of Kyle Street while the old station at Darlington Road was converted to a goods station.

On 1st September 1870 the railway from Newton Junction

eastwards to Mauchline was laid. Blackhouse and Hawkhill junctions were also created, the large triangular area between being used for engine sheds and sidings. Around the same time the Ayr Harbour Branch was laid, leaving the main line at Ayr Harbour Junction and terminating in numerous sidings at the quayside. The railway bridge across the harbour, allowing trains to reach the south quay, was erected in 1899. The Townhead Station was rebuilt from 1881 until 1886 and at that time Kyle Street east of Smith Street was closed off. Traffic was diverted up Alloway Street to the new Burns Statue Square, the statue having been erected in 1881. The extension of the railway meant the relocation of the cattle market to Castlehill Road.

The Holmston Cemetery was laid out in 1860, the large ornate gateway designed by John Murdoch being added by 1862. The cemetery has been extended a number of times since. In the cemetery are a number of notable graves, including that of George Douglas Brown, author of *The House With the Green Shutters*.

In 1877, following some large floods, the New Bridge was found to be in a dangerous condition. It was decided to demolish it and build a new crossing, costing £15,000. Relics of the old bridge survive — a panel bearing the arms of Ayr is built into the wall at Castlehill Road and some of the balusters were reused at the Pavilion.

An electricity station was built in Mill Street in the period 1896-98. This remained in burgh hands until 1923 when it was passed to the Ayrshire Electricity Board. The station was closed down in 1924 as the whole of Ayrshire was able to be supplied from the Kilmarnock power station. In 1932 Ayrshire was connected to the National Grid.

The Carnegie Library was opened on 2nd September 1893 thanks to financial help from Andrew Carnegie. Andrew Carnegie had been invited to give a lecture in the town but had to decline. Instead he offered the town £10,000 towards the cost of a library provided the burgh adopt the Free Libraries Act. This was agreed to and a magnificent building erected in Main Street. There had previously been subscription libraries in the town — the Ayr Library Society having existed in Fort Street from 1804 and the Mechanics Institution Library which was located at first in the High Street before being moved to New Bridge Street in 1852. Ayr Public Library was opened in MacNeille's Building in Newmarket Street in 1870, taking in the stock of the Library Society in 1876 and that of Newton Parish Library in 1885.

TWENTIETH CENTURY

The Boer War ceased in 1902 and the country relaxed again. Ayr lost a number of men in the battles, and in 1902 a war memorial to the men of the Royal Scots Fusiliers was erected in Burns Statue Square. The statue of a soldier was sculpted by Thomas Brock, and the names of those who died were inscribed on the pediment, recalling the wars in South Africa, Sudan, Burma and Tirah.

On 26th September 1901 the Burgh of Ayr opened its new tram-car service. The tramlines commenced at Prestwick Cross and followed Prestwick Road south to Main Street, over the New Bridge, then along High Street and south to St Leonards. A gauge of 4 feet 8½ inches was used. The tram depot was located at Bellesleyhill on Prestwick Road. On 1st June 1902 an extension south to Alloway was opened and in 1913 a branch line was laid up George Street then out Whitletts Road to the racecourse. In 1904 the town centre stretch, from Bellesleyhill to the Grammar School, was widened to double track.

The tramway ran profitably for a score or more years, but as the equipment and rails began to wear and require replacement the cost of running the service increased. Beginning to lose money, the council sold the company to the Western S.M.T. bus company who closed it down, replacing the service with buses. The last tram ran on New Year's Eve, 1931.

The Great War cost 817 men their lives, all recorded on the war memorial which was unveiled in 1924. Other memorials were erected elsewhere in the parish, such as on the wall of Alloway Village Hall and at Whitletts Cross. During the war Carrick House was used as a Red Cross Hospital, one of many large houses pressed into service. Newton Park was used as a billet, and the racecourse was converted to a training ground for the Flying Corps.

After the Great War the Department of Agriculture acquired land at Belston, Mainholm and Brickrow which was subdivided into smallholdings, with houses and steadings erected on each. Many of these smallholdings survive.

In 1919 the harbour passed into the ownership of the railway company, which made improvements before ownership was passed to the London Midland and Scottish Railway company in 1926, which in turn became British Railways in 1948. In 1950 ownership was transferred to the Docks and Inland Waterways executive, now Associated British Ports. The importation of iron ore and the export of pig iron ceased in 1928 when the ironworks at Waterside and Lugar were closed.

The ever increasing population required an improvement in the water supply, and so Loch Riecawr was added to Loch Finlas as a source in 1932. More remote than Finlas, Riecawr had its own lodgehouse and the council made an annual trip to inspect the dam. Tales abound of the amount of alcohol required to keep them warm on such visitations!

In the town centre there was much redevelopment going on as a result of the increase in the population. New houses were being built on the periphery of the town, and overcrowded and slum properties in the town centre were being demolished. Woodfield House was acquired by the council in 1919 and work commenced on building houses in its grounds. The first council houses in the town were erected in George's Avenue and let to new tenants in 1921. Lochside was acquired and plans first drawn up for a scheme there in 1924, but nothing was done until 1932, ground at Heathfield being developed beforehand.

Ayr was designated a Large Burgh in 1929, and the boundary was extended in 1935 when Whitletts, Castlehill, Alloway and Doonfoot were added. In the same year new offices were added to the rear of the County Buildings. At Whitletts, what had been a small rural village, with a large number of mining residents, was developed into a sizeable community. The old rows were gradually cleared, leaving few original buildings, other than the Primary School and the Red Stone Inn, or Manson's Pub as it was better known. In 1937 the old building of Anderson's Pub was demolished to reveal the newly-built Thistle Inn behind. A new Community Centre was opened in 1949, as was the library. Adjoining the village the lands of Dalmilling were developed, a new church being erected and a Roman Catholic chapel which was later raised to cathedral status.

The Second World War arrived in 1939, and soon plans were being made for protection in case of air raids. Hundreds of children arrived in the town from Glasgow, evacuated in case of gas attacks, but they gradually returned to the city when that fear proved to be less of a threat than at first imagined. In the burgh most open spaces were utilised for the war effort with golf courses being leased for grazing and open gardens converted into vegetable plots. At Craigie and Belleisle the mansions were requisitioned for War Office use, as was ground at Dalmilling, Dam Park, and Fulshawwood. At Doonfoot a Prisoner of War camp was created for the holding of Italians. At Spring Garden, 1941, a naval camp, known as H.M.S. "Scotia", was laid out. Also in 1941, an aeroplane crashed at Whitletts whilst taking off from the aerodrome. The flames were such that no rescue attempt could be made, and all 22 persons on board were killed. They were buried in Holmston Cemetery.

Following the resumption of peace, additional panels were added to the cenotaph, recording the 263 men who had died for their country. In the Auld Kirk a new oak pulpit was erected as a war memorial, copying the style of the original pulpit which had been removed in 1882.

Ayr has steadily grown in size since the last war. New housing estates have been formed all round the town, in places such as Doonfoot, Rozelle, Kincaidston, Holmston and Whitletts. New housing has also been erected in gap sites within the town, and large areas of Wallacetown have been rebuilt. Blocks of flats have been built in various corners of the town, often replacing older industrial or commercial buildings. Garden Court was built on the site of Mitchell's bacon factory in 1980 and Kyle Court retiral homes were built on the station sidings in 1992, Mariner's Wharf on the north harbour quayside in 1993. The tall blocks of Riverside Place, rising fourteen storeys or 140 feet were built from 1968-70 to plans by Cowie and Torry — these were reclad in 1992. Sheltered Housing units have been built in various locations throughout the town, where older residents live in smaller homes with a warden always available should something happen.

Within the town centre a number of older buildings have been removed and replaced by modern buildings. Many of these were built in a traditional style in order to preserve the general appearance of the town, others kept the original facades and built new shop premises behind, such as British Home Stores, erected in 1984, retaining facades of 1883.

John Street was altered as a major ring road, the new John Street Bridge opened on 26th August 1972 by Adam Hart, diverting north/south traffic away from the High Street and Sandgate. The Victoria Bridge had previously been reconstructed and the widened bridge opened on 19th April 1961. The main by-pass, which swings round Prestwick Airport and passes Whitletts and Holmston on its way south, was opened in stages — the first section round Monkton to Whitletts opened in 1961, south to Holmston opened in 1963 and the last stretch to Kincaidston opened in 1971. A new

town centre traffic management plan was put into operation on 28th February 1993, the High Street being restricted to buses and taxis, Sandgate and Fort Street being converted to one-way traffic.

In 1975 the Burgh Council and Ayr County Council were superseded by Strathclyde Regional Council and Kyle and Carrick District Council. The latter has its headquarters in the town, based in Burns House which had been erected in 1973. The County Buildings were used by the Regional Council as its Ayr Division headquarters. Regionalisation has not lasted too long, however, for it is planned to replace regions and districts by single-tier local authorities in 1996.

RELIGION

When the first church was founded in Ayr is not known, but it was certainly in existence by 1200, as there are references to an archdeacon at that time. It has been claimed that an earlier church, located further upstream, existed prior to the foundation of the Church of St John. Perhaps the church was relocated following the foundation of Ayr Castle. The church near the castle was a large cruciform building, with neither a spire nor a tower, but adorned with leaded glass. In the 15th century a tower was added at the west end, a means of protection by blocking off the rose window which was susceptible to attack from the sea.

Between 1219 and 1230 a group of Gilbertine followers were established at Dalmilling when Walter FitzAlan invited them to settle in Ayr. This order did not survive long, and the chapel was abandoned, the lands awarded to Paisley Abbey.

In 1230 a more successful friary operated by Dominicans or "Black" friars was established, located where the present Auld Kirk Hall stands, though a plaque indicating the approximate site is affixed to the wall of Boots' yard. Alexander II was instrumental in its foundation and granted the friars the £20 due to him from the grain mill of Ayr. In 1328 the friars had the right to get their corn ground free, and to be first in the queue at the mill. The church was dedicated to St Katherine, and St Katherine's well was long renowned for its curative powers. The Dominican monastery became very wealthy, owning extensive grounds and estates in the county.

A Franciscan or Greyfriars Monastery was established in Ayr in 1474, the friars supposedly coming at the request of the burgesses. The monastery, built in 1481 with the Pope's approval, consisted of a church, altars, belfry, dormitory, refectory, cemetery and garden. It was located on the same spot as the present Auld Kirk, and the Friar's Well was adjacent to the side of the river. During excavations on the site of British Home Stores in 1982 some carved stones from the building were discovered, indicating that it was a finely decorated edifice, with stained glass in gothic windows.

At St Leonards there existed another religious building. Dedicated to that saint, its hospital was a very ancient establishment, for by 1425 it was noted as being ruinous. It was restored and endowed that year, and from then on cared for the poor, sick and lame.

Ayrshire had by the mid 16th century strong protestant tendencies, the Lollards of Kyle being charged with heresy in 1494. John Knox preached in Ayr in 1556, and the first Protestant minister, Christopher Goodman, was appointed

The last 'Kirking of the Council' in 1975

to Ayr in 1559, one year before the full-blown Reformation. The Reformation saw the Pope's authority over the church abolished and the many Catholic images and altars destroyed. The Greyfriars and Blackfriars monasteries were demolished, friars of the former leaving the town, the latter staying on and being awarded a pension. The rights of the monasteries, such as to the mills, were transferred to the burgh.

John Porterfield was appointed as Ayr's third Presbyterian minister, and in 1600 John Welch (1568-1622) was elected his assistant. Welch was Knox's nephew, and like the reformer had a fiery zeal. He was suspended for six months for threatening rebellion against the monarch. His garden was long regarded as one of the most sacred places in Ayr, restored in 1933 but destroyed when Littlewoods' store was built in 1968. The statue which stood in it is now in the Auld Kirk. Welch became first minister in 1604, but in 1605 he was imprisoned on the Bass Rock and subsequently banished to France.

William Adair was appointed assistant to the minister in 1639, promoted to the first charge in 1644. He was a staunch Covenanter, and fought at the Battle of Mauchline Muir in 1648. He was involved in the years of struggle from then until 1682 when he was removed from the kirk for refusing to take the test, or swear allegiance to the king before the church. When he died in 1684 an ornate memorial was built into the wall of the new church erected during his term of office.

When Cromwell's troops took over the old church of St John in 1651 the people of Ayr were left with no place of worship. The Commonwealth granted the church £600 and a new church (now the Auld Kirk) was built on the site of the Greyfriars Monastery at a cost of almost £1800. In the interim the congregation had to meet in the Grammar School, at that time located in the Sandgate.

The new church was built in a typical style of its period, but was built without a tower by order of the soldiers, for fear of it being taken and being in direct conflict with the old tower of St John. T-shaped in plan, the church was opened for worship in 1656. In the same year a new gateway or lych-gate was erected across the vennel known as the Kirk Port, the original entry to the Greyfriars yard being through another close from the High Street.

Following the restoration of Charles II in 1660, and his proposals for establishing an Episcopal church in Scotland, many people in the town left the kirk and attended services held by those ministers who refused to conform. Known as Covenanters, these people were at first tolerated, but after a time laws were passed outlawing these services and putting followers under threat of execution, or at least banishment. In 1666 an insurrection broke out in Galloway and a band of men marched north to Ayr en route to Edinburgh. They were defeated at Rullion Green, Ralph Shield, merchant in Ayr, being taken prisoner and hanged in Edinburgh. Twelve other prisoners were put on trial in Ayr and eight of them were sentenced to be hanged in the town. The burgh hangman disappeared rather than perform the deed, the one from Irvine also refused, even under torture. At length it was agreed that one of the eight could go free so long as he would hang the remainder. Thus Cornelius Anderson hung the seven martyrs commemorated by the headstone in the Auld Kirkyard on 27th December 1666.

Andrew MacGill was another who suffered at Ayr in November 1684. He was buried below the gallows and a memorial formerly occupied the site, long-since gone.

In 1678 the "Highland Host" was quartered in the county with Ayr as its headquarters. This host comprised of Highland soldiers who were brought in to rout out those hillmen who refused Episcopacy. They were noted for their pillaging, and during their short spell in the burgh stole or

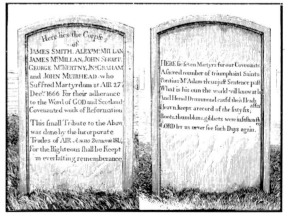

The Martyrs' Grave in Ayr Auld Kirkyard

consumed over £12,000 Scots worth of goods.

At length, in 1688, the Glorious Revolution saw James VI removed and William and Mary crowned. The religious struggles were over, and presbyterianism was adopted as the national religion of Scotland. The two Episcopal ministers in the town were removed and banned from preaching.

The church in Ayr settled down for a century thereafter, though a number of factions were created within the Established Church. The Secession of 1733 resulted in the erection of a church at the east end of King or Cross Street in 1770, the cemetery which survives being attached to the kirk. A new church was erected in George Street in 1779. These seceders were Anti-Burghers; the Burghers built a church off Wallace Street in 1799. These two groups merged in 1820 and joined the Relief Church in 1847 to form the United Presbyterian Church. The Wallace Street congregation moved to a new church erected at the north end of the New Bridge, called Darlington Place U.P. Church. However, in Ayr the Anti-burghers remained separate, at length erecting the Robertson Memorial Original Secession Church in 1901.

A Relief Church had been opened in Cathcart Street in November 1816. During construction a storm blew down the roof and part of a wall, holding up the opening. In 1847 the congregation became adherents of the United Presbyterian Church and the church was renamed Cathcart Street U.P. Church.

The New Church in Fort Street was erected in 1807-10, the Auld Kirk being too small for the membership. Similarly, in 1858 the church at Alloway was built, to serve parishioners at that end of the parish. The town continued to grow, and new Established congregations were formed in St Leonard's church, opened in 1886, and North Newton in 1885, now St James'. A mission hall of the Auld Kirk was erected in Carrick Street in 1868.

The parish of Newton-upon-Ayr was created on 15th December 1779, being disjoined from Monkton and Prestwick, the first minister appointed in 1778. Their church was located behind the Newton tolbooth, reached through a pend below the steeple. In Ayr there was also an Episcopalian congregation formed in 1743 with a church in Fullarton Street, a Moravian church in 1765 in Mill Street, and Methodist chapel in 1785, located in Charlotte Street. The Ayr Independent Congregationalists, founded in 1804, had a tabernacle in River Street, erected in 1805 and closed in 1878, the building sold to Darlington Place Church who erected their River Street Mission Hall on the site. The Evangelical Union had a congregation from 1844 and the Baptists a meeting place from 1884 when they bought the former Queen's Rooms.

The Disruption of 1843 was when many ministers and their congregations throughout Scotland left the Church of Scotland following a disagreement over patronage. In Ayr burgh the Auld and New parish kirks were virtually unaffected by this, but across the water in Wallacetown the minister and most of his congregation left that church to form their own Free Church. They met at first in William Alexander's sawmills, but by 1845 managed to erect their own new place of worship in the Sandgate. At Wallacetown a Wooden Kirk mission hall was erected for adherents who did not wish to cross the river, replaced by a new church in John Street in

1860. This Wallacetown Free Church was renamed St John's U.F. Church from 1900 until 1904, but returned to the Wallacetown name thereafter. At the Union of 1929 it was called Wallacetown South, but in 1948 it was closed, having merged with Darlington Place Church. In Newton the parish kirk congregation also split, most of the members joining the minister in the new Free Church which was erected within yards of the parish church.

The Reformed Presbyterian Church joined with the Free Church in 1876, the Cameronian members creating the Martyrs Free Church in George Street. A fifth Free Church in the town had its origins in a dispute with the Wallacetown Free Church in 1889, resulting in the creation of St Andrew's church in Park Circus in 1893.

In 1900 the United Presbyterian and Free churches nationally merged to form the United Free Church. Ayr ended up with nine U.F. churches, but the unification was not to everyone's liking. In Newton a near-riot took place in 1905 when the Free Church (Continuing) were given the Newton Free Church building (now Newton Parish), thus evicting the U.F. congregation. On 2nd July, whilst the Free congregation were inside, the U.F. congregation and about 4000 others gathered outside and it required a large police presence to disperse them. At length negotiations led to the Free congregation being given the Martyrs Church in George Street and the U.F. congregation the Main Street church.

The Trinity U.P. Church was formed in 1898, meeting at first in a hall in Midton Road. The church was added in 1902, later renamed the Church of St Columba.

In 1929 the United Free church nationally rejoined the Church of Scotland. In Ayr this resulted in fifteen congregations of the Church of Scotland. A few dissenters refused to rejoin, and formed the United Free Church (Continuing). In 1930 they built a small church for themselves in Kirkholm Avenue.

With a growing town in the post-war years new churches were built in the peripheral schemes. In St Quivox parish churches were erected at Lochside in 1940 and Dalmelling in 1953. On the south side of the river, Castlehill parish church was opened in 1958, and Kincaidston Community Church Project was commenced in 1976.

In the town centre a number of congregations were merged and some churches closed. The Darlington New Church was formed on 16th May 1948 with the merging of Darlington Place and Wallacetown South churches. In 1951 the New Kirk congregation was linked with the Auld Kirk and the church closed. However, the Cathcart Street Church acquired the building and moved there, the old church being closed. At Newton, the Old and New church congregations united on 4th July 1962, using the New Church building.

Though the Roman Catholic Emancipation Act was not passed until 1829, the Catholics in Ayr had in 1826 built for themselves a chapel dedicated to St Margaret in John Street. The Cathedral of the Good Shepherd at Dalmilling was erected from 1955-57, but was not raised to cathedral status until 1961. At Belmont, in Peggieshill Road, St Paul's Chapel was opened in 1967.

The Baptist Church in Ayr dates back to 1837, meeting at first in the Black Bull hall, Wallacetown, under Pastor Mr Morrison. Their first minister was the Revd. James Blair,

St. James Parish Church, Prestwick Road

but the congregation disbanded around 1850. A new church was founded on 21st June 1886 by 22 members, and in 1887 they acquired the former Queen's Rooms in Fort Street and converted it to a church. The Baptists established a mission on the north side of the town in 1889, resulting in the foundation of New Prestwick Baptist Church, off Prestwick Road, in 1900. A hall was added in 1961. It had 178 members in 1983, dropping to 154 in 1984. A second mission in recent years in Doonfoot and Alloway (known as the Southside Christian Fellowship) proposes the foundation of a third congregation and a new church in that district.

The Scottish Episcopal Church had a church in Ayr from 1743, building the magnificent Holy Trinity Church in Fullarton Street in 1898. The noted ecclesiastical architect, John Pearson, designer of Truro and Brisbane cathedrals, produced a Gothic design which remained incomplete. A spire and tower of 92 feet was omitted, the present tower not added until 1964 and built of precast concrete. In 1934 the church promoted the St John's Mission in James Street, but this was abandoned in 1952.

The Congregational church had two churches in Ayr for a time, belonging to different forms of congregationalism. The Morison Congregational Church acquired the former Secession Church in George Street in 1901, continuing there until 1976. The Evangelical Union Congregational Church was located in the former Anti-burgher Church in Wallace Street from 1865.

The Christian or Plymouth Brethren became quite popular in the 19th century and they established various halls in the town, including the Ebenezer Hall at Tam's Brig and the Gospel Hall in James Street. The Victoria Hall group acquired the former Wallacetown South church and opened it for worship on 14th December 1952 as the Riverside Evangelical Church. The Woodpark Evangelical Church of the Christian Brethren was built at Belmont.

The Ayrshire Christian Union had a hall in Green Street, known as the Bethel Mission. The Methodists had a church at the corner of Charlotte and Fort Streets from 1813 until 1909. Other minority groups have established places of worship over the years. Today there is an Assembly of God in Prestwick Road, a Gospel Hall in James Street, Apostolic Church in Green Street (founded 1953), Church of God in Queen Street, Church of Psychic Science at 10 Alloway Place, Church of the Nazarene (founded 1935) and a Spiritualist Church meeting in the Wallace Tower.

The Salvation Army arrived in Ayr in 1884, building a new hall in New Road in 1905, designed by Arthur Hamilton. The Mormon Church of Jesus Christ of Latter Day Saints was erected in Orchard Avenue in 1962. The Jehovah's Witnesses acquired the former Congregational Church in Wallace Street, but in November 1985 this was demolished to make way for Asda.

EDUCATION

The first school in Ayr was established at the Church of St John, though when this happened is not known. The first mention of a school in the town dates to 1233, when a dispute over land was partly judged by "Allan, master of the schools of Ayr." Nothing more is heard of a school until 1502, when Andrew MacCormyll was instructor of grammatical studies. The school still took place in the church, and it was not until 1602 that it was moved to the present site of the Academy, at that time occupied by a thatched cottage. It was extended in 1721 and 1747 and the schoolmaster's house erected in the High Street in 1773.

In the same year a second school was established near the Wallace Tower, but this was rather small and the teacher preferred to educate the pupils in his own home at the Fish Cross. There were also classes being taught below the Assembly Hall, so it was decided to erect a new building altogether. A royal charter was granted in 1798 which allowed the formation of the "Academy of Air" and work soon commenced on a classical building.

A Wallacetown School was erected in 1837 adjoining the church and in Newton a school met in the Assembly Rooms. This was rather small, but had to suffice until a new building was erected in Green Street in 1847, known as Newton Academy.

That education was still tied to religion resulted in other denominations forming their own schools. One of the earliest was the Moravians, who established a school in Mill Street in 1816. Soon after the Roman Catholic Emancipation Act the Catholics built their own school at St Margaret's. The Episcopalians erected a school next to the Trinity Church around 1840, continuing to educate children there until 1907. The Disruption of 1843 resulted not only in the foundation of Free Churches, but also Free Church Schools, at the Fish Cross, Newton Free Church and Weaver Street.

In addition to the church-run schools there were a number of private schools, financed entirely on fees paid by the pupils. William Watson ran one such school in Content Street, known as Wallacetown Academy. This continued to operate until Watson's retiral in the 1850s. A Charlotte Street Academy existed in the 19th century.

Those who could not afford the school fees could still find some education in the charity schools. In 1825 John Smith left money for the establishment of a school for poor children. Known as Smith's Institution, this had its origins in the poorshouse but in 1842 a new building was erected at the head of Kyle Street in what became known as Smith Street. Another charity school existed in Charlotte Street, opened in 1843 following the gift of money from Archibald Hamilton of Rozelle. Lady Jane Hamilton's School, as it was named, educated around 250 pupils from Ayr, Newton and Wallacetown.

Ayr Grammar School was established in 1867 following a public meeting which called for the creation of a "middle school", with fees lower than that of the Academy, but in excess of Smith's Institution. The school, erected near the Horsemarket, cost £1300 to build and was opened in 1868.

In 1872 the Education (Scotland) Act brought most of the schools in the burgh under local authority control and soon education was compulsory for children aged between 5 and 13. School Boards were established to run the schools, and many new buildings were erected at this time. Newtonhead Public School was built in 1874 to replace the two Free Church schools north of the river. A new Wallacetown School was erected in 1875 at the foot of Queen Street; Smith's Institution moved to a new building in Holmston Road in 1884 (renamed Holmston School in 1930); Russell Street School was opened in 1890. The Academy was extended in 1880 as was Lady Jane Hamilton's School. The schools for orphans were rebuilt as Schools of Industry, one for boys and another for girls. These were erected at St Leonard's.

Not all schools were passed over to the School Board. The Roman Catholic school at St Margaret's and the Episcopalian School remained independent. St Margaret's School was extended from Elba Street to new premises off Whitletts Road in 1893. In 1909 the school at the chapel was closed, the Whitletts Road school extended to accommodate all Catholic pupils. At 22 Wellington Square the Wellington School remained private, and Newnham House School operated in Fullarton Street.

Ayr Landward School Board covered the remainder of the parish outwith the burgh. It erected a new Alloway Public School in 1896. St Quivox School Board ran the little school in St Quivox and also the subscription school in Whitletts, opened in the 1850s. This was replaced by a new Whitletts Public School in 1909.

In October 1899, the schools in the parish had the following rolls:

Russell Street School	1,133
Newtonhead	744
Netwon Academy	551
Ayr Academy	c. 450
Wallacetown	418
St Margaret's R.C. schools	408
Ayr Grammar School	406
Smith's Institution	363
Trinity Episcopalian School	322
Lady Jane Hamilton's School	256
Alloway Public School	c. 120
Whitletts Public School	c. 120
St Quivox School	c. 65

In 1905 Newton Park School was opened by the School Board and the Grammar School and Newton Academy rebuilt in 1909 and 1911 respectively. Heathfield School was opened in 1931.

In 1947 education again received a reorganisation when the leaving age was raised to fifteen. The Ayr County Education Committee had to build new schools to supplement or replace overcrowded buildings, seven thousand pupils being educated in twelve schools. Ayr Academy was changed into a selective secondary school, taking the better pupils from a wider district, entry being restricted by a qualifying examination. For those who failed to get in, Junior Secondary schools were available — Ayr Grammar, Newton Academy, Newton Park and Russell Street schools. Newton Academy was closed in 1980, being used as Ayr Academy's Technical Annexe until being converted to the Newton Advisers' and Education Resource Centre.

The younger children were educated at what became known as Primary schools. These were created at Ayr Grammar, Newton Academy, Heathfield, Newtonhead, Wallacetown, Whitletts, Holmston and Alloway. In 1951 Braehead Primary School was opened, Dalmilling Primary School in 1959, Forehill in 1968, Castlehill in 1968, Doonfoot in 1974 and Kincaidston in 1975. The primary schools at Newtonhead, Newton Park and Russell Street were closed in 1984 when Newton Primary School opened in a modern building. In 1993 Castlehill Primary School was scheduled for closure despite a campaign by parents and pupils.

Nursery Schools became fashionable in the post-war years, and nursery provision has grown over the years. Wallacetown Nursery School was established in 1952 in the former Wallacetown School in Queen Street. At Dalmilling, Westwood Nursery School was opened in 1977. Playgroups such as those at Whitletts and Rozelle have also become popular.

With the increase in population and raising of the school age to sixteen, new secondary schools were created in the town to cope with the numbers. Belmont Academy, built to accommodate 1645 pupils had its first session in 1960, and Mainholm Academy was opened in 1965. Kyle Academy was built at Holmston farm in 1979. Since 1968 Ayr Academy has been a comprehensive school.

The Catholic church still held influence over St Margaret's School, though control was passed to the Education Authority in 1918. Initially, those who wished to continue their education beyond the age of fifteen had to travel either to St Joseph's in Kilmarnock (boys) or St Michael's in Irvine (girls). In 1966 Queen Margaret Academy was established at Mainholm, but in January 1976 a new building was opened at Kincaidston, built to accommodate 1250 pupils. St Margaret's and St John's were primary schools, and St Catherine's Primary School was created in 1957 but in 1988 it moved into the old Queen Margaret building and was renamed Good Shepherd School.

Special education provision in Ayr dates to 1918 when a special school was opened in Green Street Lane. This was replaced when St Leonard's School was established in the former Girls' Industrial School. Special Education provision was divided into three levels in 1980 when Southpark School was opened for children with serious difficulties and Craigpark School opened for those with profound learning difficulties. St Leonard's Special School continued in the old building until Rosebank School was built and opened in 1987.

Private education was catered for by Cambusdoon School and Newnham House School for boys and Wellington School for girls. Cambusdoon operated between 1926 and 1967, Newnham House from the 19th century until after the war, the girls' school founded in Wellington Square in 1839, moved to Carleton Turrets in 1923, and expanding thereafter.

Craigie College of Education was built in 1964 on the lands of Craigie House. Primary school teachers were taught here, but with a fall in demand the college was under threat of closure until it became the Education Faculty of Paisley University.

Ayr Technical College was established in new premises at the Dam Park in 1966, replacing older technical schools which dated from the early 1940s, located in the former Boys' Industrial School. The name has since been shortened to Ayr College and an annexe formed in Cumnock.

HEALTH

In Mill Vennel a hospital was erected in 1604 using stone from the Greyfriars monastery. The church and burgh council collaborated in the foundation, £350 being spent on the building. Only patients who could recite the Lord's Prayer were admitted.

The first proper hospital to be built in Ayr was the General Voluntary or Fever Hospital which was erected in its own grounds at the junction of Smith and Mill streets. Built in 1844, it had twenty beds.

A small hospital for the care of cholera and smallpox victims was established in the Heathfield area in 1856. This was a corrugated iron building, containing six beds, where infected patients could be kept isolated.

The district lunatic asylum was opened in 1869. Known originally as the Glengall Asylum, it was renamed the Ailsa Hospital. It was designed by Charles Edward (1816-1890) who got the contract following a competition. He belonged to Dundee, and there designed the Royal Dundee Liff Hospital for the same purpose.

In 1883 the County Hospital was erected in Holmston Road, replacing the Fever Hospital. It had 44 beds for general patients and twenty beds for fever sufferers.

In 1903 a small rural hospital was created at Crofthead which was designed to specialise in the treatment of Smallpox. Previously this disease had been treated in a "wholly unsuitable" wooden building located in the grounds of the County Hospital. Crofthead Hospital, however, also dealt with ear, nose and throat problems of children from 1937-44.

In 1905 Heathfield Infectious Diseases Hospital was opened to the north of the town. It required an interlocutor by the Court of Session to compel the Burgh of Ayr to provide the buildings, the only such case occurring in Scotland. Five acres of land were developed as a hospital, with separate buildings for each disease. It cost £21,000 to create the hospital and it dealt with 138 patients within its first year. In 1937 a Nurses Home and venereal disease clinic were opened. An out-patient department was built in 1962, now converted to Heathfield Clinic.

Seafield House was acquired by the County Council in 1920 and converted to a maternity and children's hospital. In 1944 it was converted to a hospital for sick children only. As a replacement, the Thorneyflat Maternity Hospital was erected from 1939 until 1944 by Ayr Town Council. This hospital was closed in the late 1980s and the building demolished.

In 1948 the National Health Service was created and it took over the operation of the local hospitals. An ambulance service was then introduced, the depot located at Fraser's garage in Fullarton Street. This served the town until 1959 when a new depot was opened in Annpit Road. This was replaced in June 1984 with new headquarters, expanding to a new building next door in 1992.

The new Ayr Hospital was erected on a greenfield site to the south of the Ailsa Hospital. This massive brick building, with accommodation for 301 patients on opening was designed

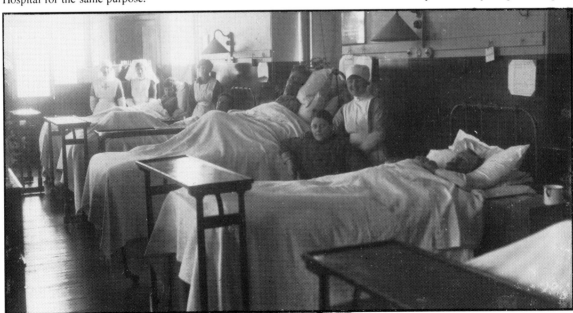

A ward at the County Hospital

by Keppie Henderson architects and was opened in 1991 having cost £31 million to build. On 1st April 1992 it became part of one of the first two Scottish Hospital Trusts.

Private medical care in the county was boosted in 1992 when the Carrick Glen Hospital was opened. Erected at Glenparks farm on the Dalmellington road, the hospital is owned by the Independent British Hospital Association.

The Ayrshire Hospice was opened in 1989 in what had been Gargowan House in Racecourse Road, dating from around 1820. Five years of fund-raising had gone on prior to the conversion and extension of the house, ideally suited for the care of the terminally ill.

INDUSTRY

Fishing has been carried on from the mouth of the river since earliest times, and continues to this day. Associated with the fishing industry was a ropeworks, located on the Newton side of the harbour and existing from before 1775.

The harbour was improved in 1839 and 1855, with dredging operations taking place and the quays rebuilt. The dock on the north side was excavated from the solid rock between 1874-81.

The harbour remains a busy port, used for the transportation of coal to Ireland, export of whisky to America and the importation of rum. The fishmarket on the south side of the river is still used by the inshore fishing boats, a number of which are based in the town, though some are registered as having Dunure as their home port. The selling of the catch is undertaken by Ivan Boardley.

The manufacture of ships and boats was carried out in Ayr for a number of years prior to the creation of a dry-dock and shipbuilding yard on the North Harbour. The shipyard on the south side of the river, with its dock running parallel with the shore, was constructed in 1881, the Ailsa Shipbuilding Company taking it over in 1902.

Coal mining in Ayr parish is first noted at Alloway in 1528. By the 17th century shafts had been sunk within the town to work the coal which was used for limekilns or for export. Drainage was a problem, particularly near the coast, and it was not until the later 18th century when steam engines were used for pumping water out of the shafts that the mines began to grow. Armstrong's map of 1775 shows coal pits with a steam engine along the Newton shore, with a waggonway running to the harbour. A second is located at Wallacetown, at what is now the junction of King and Queen streets, with a waggon way running down to the river and along the bank to the Auld Brig. A third coal pit with steam engine existed near Viewfield Road.

In 1840 there were a number of pits on the north side of the river, all owned by George Taylor & Co. Allison Pit was located at Russell Street, Newtonhead Pit was situated near Tam's Brig, Saltfield Pit and Green Pit were near Newton Lodge. Two new pits were sunk north of Craigie House around 1850 and other pits existed at Whitletts and Auchincruive, a "Waggon Road" (hence the street-name) being used to haul the coal by horses to the North Quay.

The last mines to exist in the parish were those of Glenburn and Mossblown, the former near Prestwick, the latter at Mossblown near Annbank. Glenburn Colliery, the last of the local pits, was closed in 1973.

The casting of metals became a prosperous industry in the town. In 1857 there were three foundries in Newton. By 1909 there were at least five foundries in Ayr, located in Smith Street (Kyle Iron Foundry owned by John M. Rodger), Limond's Wynd (Wallacetown Foundry owned by Robert Hunter and Sons), York Street (Vulcan Iron Foundry owned by J. & T. Young), High Street (Ayr Brass Foundry) and the Carrick Brassworks owned by Archibald Welsh in John Street. At Green Street Lane James Thomson & Sons, blacksmiths and structural engineers, were founded in 1880.

In 1900 a forge and stampworks were set up in West Sanquhar Road in the newly-erected Neptune Works. This company made forgings for shipbuilding but after 1914 much of its business went to the vehicle industry. Known as the Scottish Stamping and Engineering Company, it became part of GKN. The Wallacetown Engineering Company moved to Heathfield from Viewfield Road, and was later taken over by Simplex then Allenwest. The company makes electrical control equipment for mines throughout the world, developing their own kind of hinge which makes them a world-beater. The Victoria or "Wee Stampworks" of James Dickie in Somerset Road was added to by a new Heathfield Foundry at Seaforth Road. At the north-east end of the Auld Brig, next to River Terrace, was Speirs' iron plane works. At the Townhead John Wallace & Sons' agricultural machinery works was opened in 1904. Scottish Mechanical Light Industries opened its Ayr factory in 1946.

W.G. Walker was founded in 1811 and set up the Hawkhill Chemical Works in Somerset Road to produce asphalt for roofing purposes. The chemical fertiliser works on Newton Shore were established in 1860 by A. Weir & Co. in the former Miller's Foundry. Daniel Wyllie & Co. took over in 1880, and the firm remained in their hands until 1928 when it was sold to Scottish Agricultural Industries. At River Terrace was Hyland's Starch Works, closed at the turn of the century. William Alexander's Sawmills were located in John Street; the continuation of that street to the Victoria Bridge required the removal of the mills to Heathfield. James Paton had a second sawmill on the south side of the harbour from 1837 until 1881 when they moved to a new site off York Street. William Paton, building contractors, was founded in 1867, Donald McLean in 1932 but going into receivership in 1991. William Johnston, painter and decorator, commenced business in 1839.

The woollen industry is also long-established. In 1827 James Templeton bought the wool mill in Fort Street (at the corner with Charlotte Street) and there commenced carpet manufacture in 1832. He extended by adding a dye house in Mill Street. The works in Fort Street produced carpets up until 1876 when it was destroyed by fire. Instead of rebuilding on what was a cramped site, a new yellow-brick factory was built in Mill Street, opening in 1878 and continuing to work until around 1970. Alexander Begg's woollen factory in Viewfield Road was established around 1900. Near to it is the Belvidere Mill of British Replin, formerly a lace factory.

William Gray's carpet factory was located at McCall's Avenue, the company founded in 1876. There were plans to greatly extend it in 1948 but it was closed in 1974 with the loss of 1100 jobs.

In 1838 there were 1087 cotton and wool looms weaving cloth for Glasgow and Paisley agents. This had increased from 100 wool weaving looms and 15 stocking weavers which existed in 1776. A large number of Irish people were employed in the trade, and many single-storey weavers' cottages were erected around the town, notably in Newton.

Brewing has been carried on in the burgh for centuries. In 1775 a brewery existed in Mill Vennel and another in the middle of the fort. The longest surviving company was Turner's Ayr and Newton Breweries Limited, founded in 1789, having breweries in Mill Street and at 108-110 Main Street. A.M. Turner gifted the money for the erection of a steel bridge across the River Ayr in 1900, not only as a gift to the people of Ayr, but also to allow his employees easier access from their homes on the north side of the river. The company latterly specialised in making lemonade. Another aerated water manufacturer was Carey, but that company was taken over by Curries of Auchinleck. Robert Forrest's tea and whisky blending company was formed in 1828, having a shop at 62 High Street and a bonded warehouse in Kyle Street. His "Flowers of the 'Forrest'" whisky was popular in the Victorian period.

The tanning industry started in a small way, but by 1837 there were three sizeable tanneries in the town, with two hundred men making footwear. Harry Beebee's tannery was located in Mill Street, the last such business in the town, only recently being demolished. Andrew Lees established a large boot and shoe factory in McCall's Avenue, known as the St Crispin Works after the patron saint of cobblers. Alexander Cuthbert also had a factory in McCall's Avenue, at Britannia Place, known as Newton Leather Works, opened in 1883. R. Dobbie and Company had been boot and shoe makers since 1830, also having a tannery in Mill Street. James Allan have sold shoes since 1783.

The sugar industry in Ayr was relatively short-lived. The sugar house, of seven storeys, was built in 1772 on the promontory beyond the fort. The trade only survived for a few years, there being proposals in 1790 to change its use to a cotton spinning factory, but in 1794 it was converted to Ayr Barracks.

Robert Carty had a tobacco pipe factory at Clunes Vennel, established in 1857. Walter Mitchell & Sons had a large bacon curing business in Main Street, later moving to Heathfield. The American Steam Laundry was established in 1891. At Alloway Street James Milroy operated as a florist since 1876.

In 1967 an industrial estate was created at Heathfield Road, many of the older industries which were located on cramped sites in the town centre moving out to the level ground. New industries were attracted, and a number of commercial yards and businesses were set up. In 1993 a new retail park for large out of town shops and superstores was built.

The industrial estate at Mosshill owes its origin to the demise of the coal industry in the Doon valley. It had been planned to create an industrial estate in the vale, but the narrowness of it made this restrictive, so instead Mosshill was developed. The first factory to open there was Prestwick Circuits, followed by Digital Equipment, both companies quickly expanding.

Street Vendors in the High Street at the turn of the Century

COMMERCE

Ayr has been a market centre for centuries, attracting shoppers from the east and south of the county, as well as tourists from further afield during the summer months.

Back in the 16th century or earlier, the shops or booths stocked far less of a selection, supplying mainly the basics required for living. Market stances were created at various points in the street the Fish Cross being located at the junction of High and Old Bridge streets, the Malt Cross where the High Street joins the Sandgate. The Meal Market was located at the south side of the Tolbooth until 1843, now occupied by the Winton Buildings branch of the Clydesdale Bank. Next to it was the Web (from the weavers' term for a woven fabric) Market and the Wool Market. The cattle market was located at what was known as the Fauldbacks, a location now occupied by Smith Street, and the Horse Market was adjacent.

These street markets were gradually replaced by new trading locations, both to clear the streets and to get more space. The Buttermarket Hall off the High Street was erected in 1869, replacing the older Buttermarket which had been located in Newmarket Street since 1814. The Corn Exchange was located off the High Street as were the Fish and Vegetable markets. The slaughter house stood at the south-east end of Mill Street, erected in 1747. A Flesh Market was added beside it in 1764. In 1801 a new Fish Market was built at the harbour.

Some of the shops and businesses in the town have quite early origins. Perhaps the oldest is Whighams, importers and distributors of wine. The company was founded in 1766 as Alexander Oliphant, bringing wines from all corners of the world, in some cases smuggling it ashore to avoid taxation.

Affleck's of Ayr, furniture manufacturers and sellers, were founded in 1810, having their factory and shop in the High Street until 1988; P.B. Hill, fishmongers and game dealers, operated from 1815 until 1961; Alexander Imrie, seed merchant, commenced business in 1820; William Galbraith, baker, started in 1844; Alexander Cuthbert, children's footwear specialist, originated in 1845; H.A. MacBride, grocer in Elba Street, originated in 1853; A. Picken, butcher, dates from 1870.

Matthew Mark, jeweller, opened for business in 1863 at 11 Newmarket Street, with competition from Wallace Allan in 1873, David Logan in 1897 and Henry Lyall in the 1920s. James Fraser opened in 1902, developing into Frasers outdoor equipment suppliers, with branches in Stranraer, Dumfries, Lanark and Hawick. Stephen and Pollock, bookseller and publisher, located in the Sandgate, was closed in 1975. S. Irvine and Sons, bookseller, commenced in 1832, with premises in "Ye Olde Tolboothe" at 75 High Street. Ogg the chemist in Newmarket Street was founded in 1836.

The Carrick Furniture House was founded in 1888; it later owned the largest furniture warehouse in Britain at Catrine mill. Andrew Hay and Company also had a house furnishing business and electrical shop at 252 High Street, established in 1930. In Boswell Park was James Gilchrist's Land o' Burns Bakeries. West Coast Fisheries were established in 1935 with premises in Newmarket Street; Brownlie's florists in 1932.

In 1896 David Hourston opened his department store in Alloway Street, bringing a new style of shopping to the town. This was taken over by the House of Fraser in 1949 and renamed Arnotts, but in 1989 became independent again, owned by McMaster Stores and trading under the Hourston name. The company went into liquidation in January 1993 but has since been taken over.

The Co-op movement arrived in Ayr with a branch of the Kilmarnock Equitable Co-operative Society being opened in South Harbour Street in 1896. Further premises were added in Allison Street in 1898 and Main Street in 1899. A bakery was erected in McCall's Avenue in 1908. In 1916 a new building containing shops and houses was opened in George Street, costing £5000 and designed by William Valentine. The movement began to fade after the Second World War, the last co-op to close in Ayr was the shop in Main Street which ceased trading in 1984.

Multi-national shops arrived in Ayr with the opening of Woolworths and Boots in 1925. Marks and Spencer followed in 1935. Littlewoods was opened in 1969, Safeway in 1974, the new Marks and Spencer in the same year (requiring the demolition of the oldest house in Ayr, Blair's tenement, which dated from the 15th century), British Home Stores in 1983, and Gateway (now Asda) in 1987.

Modern shopping centres were opened with no traffic to disturb the customers. The Lorne Arcade was opened around 1900, later known as the Central Arcade, but recently returning to its original name following renovations in 1991. The Dalblair Arcade was opened in 1967, the Kyle Centre in 1988. To assist in the same way, Newmarket and Carrick streets were pedestrianised in 1980. Some of the larger shops were subdivided into smaller units, the indoor market becoming common. These were created at the Forum centre (High Street), and Dalblair Road.

The current trend is towards out-of-town shopping facilities, car-parking in the town centre being something of a problem. Tesco opened its new store at the Racecourse in 1991, the old Boswell Park shop, erected as recently as 1974, being demolished and replaced with a car park. A new Safeway opened at the market site in Castlehill Road in 1994 and proposals exist for a Sainsbury at the Whitletts roundabout.

All these shoppers and traders require banks, and most banking companies have had branches in the town over the years. Douglas, Heron & Co. was founded in 1769 and was known as the Ayr Bank. It was a financial failure, suspending payment in 1772 causing widespread distress, many landowners having to sell their properties in order to cover their liabilities. The Ayrshire Banking Company was set up in 1830, but was taken over by the Western Bank in 1845. It failed in 1857.

In New Bridge Street was the North of Scotland Bank (1909), Western Bank of Scotland and the National Bank of Scotland; in the Sandgate the Bank of Scotland, Ayr Savings Bank (founded 1909, later the City of Glasgow Savings Bank and now the Trustee Savings Bank, removed to the High Street), Commercial Bank and Royal Bank. In the High Street the Union Bank of Scotland, Clydesdale Bank in Winton Buildings (replacing the branch in Newmarket Street in 1856) and others. The British Linen Bank was located at the junction of Miller Road with Killoch Place. Other banks included the Mercantile Bank of Scotland (1903), and more recent companies such as the NWS Bank in High Street and National Westminster Bank in Miller Road. The Girobank was available at post offices. Another means of saving which has developed is the building society, there being nine different societies represented in the town in 1993 plus numerous agencies for others.

Following the growth in popularity of automobiles, garage premises were founded by William Young in Carrick Street in 1921 (demolished in 1992), and by Robert McCall in Galloway Avenue in 1948. Many other service stations, car showrooms and associated businesses have come and gone over the decades.

To accommodate the influx of visitors wishing to view the Burns country or else to do business in the town, a number of hotels have been opened over the years. Old coaching inns were the Black Bull Hotel in River Street and the King's Arms Hotel in the High Street which had stabling behind it, reached through the archway from New Bridge Street. The hotel was demolished in 1925. Milrig House in Charlotte Street was converted to a hotel in 1860 and demolished in 1970. The Ayrshire and Galloway Hotel was opened in 1896. The Queen's Hotel was located in South Harbour Street. The Ayr Arms Hotel in the High Street, better known as Matha Dickie's, was the last pub to survive in the High Street, the bar closed in 1985. Since then, however, another pub has opened. At the turn of the century there had been around twenty licensed premises in the High Street, the street numbers being changed over the years.

9 Prince of Wales Tavern
12 King's Arms Hotel
48 Eagle Tavern

52 Vulcan Tavern
61 Cross Keys Inn
64 Queens Head Inn
65 Welcome Tavern
78 Osborne Hotel
83 Jeanie Muir's
97 George Inn
101 Crown Inn
104 Star Inn - 19th century coaching hostelry.
120 Blue Bell Inn
124 George Spier's
130 Mason's Arms Inn
159 Whip Inn - owned by Society of Whipmen
     1818-1948.
174 James Cleat's
191 James Cochrane's
209 Ayr Arms Hotel - Matthew Dickie's
214 William Gold's
219 Alexander MacLean's
230 Tam o' Shanter Inn
231 John Goudie & Son
237 William MacKissock's
241 Plough Inn
245 Sun Inn

Relying originally on purely Burns followers, the Burns Monument Hotel at Alloway was opened in 1829. Likewise an old inn in the High Street, known as the Plough Inn, was renamed the Tam o' Shanter Inn to benefit from the supposed connection with the famous poem.

As the Victorian period arrived, many new hotels were opened and a number of large houses converted to hotels to cater for the growing number of tourists flocking to the coast from Glasgow and beyond. Dalblair House became the Hotel Dalblair. Redhouse (renamed Savoy Park), Sea Tower, St Andrews and many others were all converted from houses to hotels. Many large houses in Wellington Square, Miller Road and other streets in the First Ward were likewise changed to hotels or guest houses. With the redevelopment of the railway station, the large Station Hotel was opened in 1886. For those who disliked alcohol, the Anchor Temperance Hotel was located at the junction of Fort and Harbour streets. The Heads of Ayr Hotel was opened in 1948.

The Caledonian Hotel in Dalblair Road was opened in 1971, rising seven storeys in height and containing 114 bedrooms, five bars and two restaurants. Today there are over fifty hotels in the town, plus many more guest houses and bed and breakfast establishments. The Palm Court Hotel in Racecourse View was in 1948 converted to a convalescent home for SOGAT, renamed Morrison Court. A number of other eventide or nursing homes have been established, such as Cumnor Hall, Auchenbeg House, Blair Lodge, Glenfairn House and Nether Auchendrane.

RECREATION

The Low Green is perhaps one of the oldest places of recreation in Ayr, the grounds being gifted by Royal Charter to the burgh sometime in the 14th century. It has been used for numerous sports over the centuries, from horse-racing to football, but today is basically an open stretch of grass, much beloved by holidaymakers.

Other parks in the town were either acquired by the burgh or else gifted to the residents by various benefactors. Craigie estate was bought by the council in 1940, the grounds partially developed by the College of Education. The nearby Dam Park was acquired in 1948, having been the location of the "Pageant of Ayrshire" in 1934.

Belleisle was bought in 1925 for £25,000 and the two golf courses opened a couple of years later. Cambusdoon was acquired in 1967 and Rozelle was gifted in 1968. At the latter park the Maclaurin Art Galleries were opened in 1976. The money for these was bequested by Mary Ellen Maclaurin of Dunellan in Wheatfield Road in memory of her husband, James Henry Maclaurin, who died in 1919. Dalmilling golf course was created in 1960. Corsehill House, which stood in Monument Road and was erected around 1830, was bought by the council and demolished in the 1960s, the gardens being retained by the parks department and open to the public.

Horse racing was popular prior to the establishment of a proper race course to the south of the town in 1787. This was closed in 1906 when the New Racecourse was opened in Whitletts Road. Here the Scottish Grand National and Western Meeting form two of the major competitions.

Football has been played in Ayr since the second half of the 19th century. Ayr Thistle Football Club played on the Low Green as early as 1872, but at that time the game was still mixed with Rugby rules. The Thistle reached the Scottish Cup semi-finals in 1877, being beaten 9-0 by the Vale of Leven. Ayr Eglinton was founded in 1875, playing at the Old Racecourse, but in 1876 it merged with Ayr Academy's team to form Ayr Academicals. In 1879 the Academicals and Thistle merged to form Ayr F.C., playing at Springvale Park. They moved to Beresford Park in 1884, and to Somerset Park in 1888. Parkhouse F.C. was founded in 1886, within two years taking Beresford Park as their home ground when Ayr F.C. had moved on to Somerset. In 1910 the two teams joned together to form Ayr United, playing at Somerset Park.

United, or the "Honest Men" as they are known, won the Second Division in 1913 and were promoted to the First Division, remaining there until 1925. They have won the Second Division title seven times in total. This included season 1927-28 when Jimmy Smith broke the record for league goals, scoring 66. In 1973 the club reached the Scottish Cup semi-finals, being beaten by Rangers 2-0 at Hampden in front of a crowd of 51,158.

Other teams which have played in the town include Ayr Victoria, Ayr Albert, Ayr Fort, Ayr Bonnie Doon, Newton Rovers, Whitletts Victoria, Ayr Boswell Boys Club. Of these Whitletts Victoria deserves more than just a mention. The Vics played at various grounds before settling at Voluntary Park which was opened in 1949. The club won the second division of the Ayrshire league in 1980, 1982 and 1986, but folded in 1992. The club was reformed in 1993.

Ayr Rugby Football Club was formed in 1899, playing initially on the Low Green, followed by Northfield, the Dam Park, Old Racecourse, and King George V playing fields. On 20th November 1962 the club purchased the market garden of Millbrae and there laid out a new pitch, the farmhouse converted to a clubhouse. On 28th April 1979 the club played a "British Lions" team to mark the opening of the new

The Beach and Esplanade

was converted to a cinema called the Ayr Electric Pavilion. This cinema was rebuilt in 1931 as Green's Playhouse, but has since been converted to a bingo hall.

Other cinemas were opened in the heyday of the film industry, giving the townsfolk a choice of seven or more places where movies were shown. Ayr Picture Palace existed in Burns Statue Square from 1910 (located in the Drill Hall of 1902), later the Palace Cinema, but this was closed when purpose built cinemas were erected and was converted to the Palais de Danse dance hall, later Bobby Jones' Ballroom. A Picture House opened in the High Street in 1921, later known as the Gaumont. The Orient Picture House in Newton Main Street was opened in 1932, the Regal in Prestwick Road in 1933. The Ritz Cinema in New Road opened in 1936 and the Odeon in Burns Statue Square, the only cinema in town which survives as such, was opened on 30th July 1938, the architect being Andrew Mather. In 1987 the Odeon was converted to a three-screen cinema, a fourth added in 1990. Films were also shown for a time in the Town Hall, Wallace Tower and the Unionist Club in New Road.

For lovers of the stage, the Caledonian Theatre was opened in a wooden building in Carrick Street in 1895. This survived until September 1902 when the Gaiety Theatre was opened. However, the first Gaiety was destroyed by fire in 1903 and had to be rebuilt. "The New Gaiety Theatre" produced the first "Gaiety Whirl" in 1931. Ben Popplewell ran the theatre from 1925 until his death in 1950, his sons Eric and Leslie continuing until 1973. In 1972 it was

500 seater stand.

Cricket was played on ground at the north end of the Doonfoot Bridge, on the lands of Gearholm, in the early 1900s. Ayr Cricket Club, founded in 1859, played at first on the Low Green, moving to the cattle market park in 1883, to Northfield in 1888 and to the Dam Park in 1898 prior to moving to Cambusdoon in 1935. During the 1860s there were no fewer than five senior cricket clubs in the town. Victoria Cricket Club played at the Racecourse.

Tennis clubs were formed in Ayr and Castlehill, the former playing on the courts created in the middle of the citadel.

Curling was at one time one of the most popular sports followed by men in their free time. Curling ponds were created at various places, including Mainholm Tilework, Slaphouse Burn at Rozelle, Old Racecourse, Castlehill Pond and Townhead. Winters seem to have become less severe over the years, and the sport lost its popularity. However, with the opening of Ayr Ice Rink a number of teams moved indoors, and the game survives in the present ice rink.

Cycling became a very popular form of relaxation in the early 20th century. The Ayr Roads Club was formed in 1933 and its members toured all over the country and beyond. One of its founder members, David Bell, achieved a greater fame from his articles in the "Ayrshire Post" under the pen-name "The Highwayman". A memorial was erected to him at Rowantree Toll in his beloved Galloway Hills. His articles have been collected into two books. Cycle-racing also took place, there being stadiums at Boswell Park, known as Carrick Street Oval, and from 1897 until 1924 at Somerset Park, surrounding the football pitch, the cycle track being described as "one of the finest in Scotland".

The Ayr Entertainment and Roller Skating Rink was erected in Boswell Park in the early 1900s, a rather simple arched hall with an abundance of pseudo-classical fenestrations on the entrance front. The building catered for the craze of roller skating at the time, but in October 1910

Auld Brig o' Doon

threatened with closure, but the council acquired it and the popular shows continued. Theatre-going was so popular that in 1944 the old Robertson Memorial Church in Craigie Road was bought by the council and converted to the Civic Theatre.

In 1939 the Ayr Ice Rink was opened in Beresford Terrace. Home to the popular Ayr Raiders ice hockey team in the 1950s, the rink was closed in 1973 and the building replaced by a Safeway supermarket. A new ice rink was opened in Limekiln Road in 1974. Ice hockey continued to be represented by Ayr Bruins, but they were disbanded in 1992.

In 1943 the Tam o' Shanter Inn was purchased by the council but remained in use as an inn until 1957 when it was converted into a museum of memorabilia associated with Robert Burns. The building reverted to its former use in 1993.

Each year a reconstructed ride follows the route taken by Tam from one of Ayr's hostelries to the Auld Brig at Alloway. Tam probably did not leave this inn, but it is it which is used as the starting point. Also created for Burns lovers was the Land o' Burns Centre at Alloway. Opened in 1976, the centre has an audio-visual theatre, gift shop, tearoom, gardens and parking.

In 1960 the Dam Park Hall was built, used for various sporting events, exhibitions and conferences and the Gaelic Mod in 1973. The Ayr Flower Show was held here until it outgrew the building, moving to large marquees which were erected at Rozelle from 1987. The Ayr Motor Show was also held in the hall until it moved on to Prestwick Airport. The Ayr Agricultural Show was held on the lands of the Dam Park

from 1852 until 1946 when it moved to the New Racecourse. It has gradually grown since, becoming the second largest agricultural show in the country. In June 1958 the Royal Highland Show was held on the Old Racecourse when that show was still held at different places prior to settling at Ingliston.

The former naval base at the Heads of Ayr was in 1947 taken over by Butlin's and converted to a holiday camp. They had previously tried to develop the Low Green. Over 3,500 visitors can be accommodated here every week. In 1988 the holiday camp was given a new image, and reopened as Wonderwest World.

The new swimming baths were erected at South Harbour Street in 1972. There had previously been plans to build them at Wallace Street and even earlier, in the 1930s, proposals for an outdoor pool similar to Prestwick's, but these came to nought.

Many clubs and societies have been founded in the town over the centuries. Many were groups associated with a particular sport, hobby or religion, others being self-help or friendly societies. The Y.M.C.A. had a meeting place at 138 High Street. The Masons had a number of lodges in the town, building a temple in Nile Court in 1895. This was occupied by St Paul's Lodge, number 204, founded in 1799. Lodge St James 125 at Newton on Ayr was founded in 1771. The Ayr County Club was formed in 1872 and built premises at 41 Sandgate, now the Queen's Court Centre. At Newton the Conservative Working Men's Club was erected in 1891, designed by James Morris. The foundation stone was laid by Lord Halsbury, Lord High Chancellor of Great Britain. The building is now the premises of "Safe North Ayr".

THE AULD BRIG—If it had not been for Burns' poem "The Brigs of Ayr" this 15th century bridge would have been demolished long ago. Having four arches and large cutwaters, the bridge is first mentioned in the Burgh Charters in 1440. In 1491 King James IV passed over the bridge and gifted ten shillings to the masons working on it. The Auld Brig was restored between 1907-10 at a cost of £10,000, and plaques on it record the donations from Burns followers. This view was taken from the north side of the river with the Wallace Tower and Townhead factory chimneys visible.

NEWTON CASTLE—This engraving of 1693 by Captain John Slezer seems to be the only illustration of Newton Castle. The tower, which stood where Asda car-park is now, was owned by the Wallaces of Craigie, followed by the Hamiltons. A typical Scots tower house, the castle was L-shaped in plan, perhaps built in two stages. It dates from before 1440, when the lands of Newton in Kyle Stewart are noted. The Barony of Sanquhar was created in 1530, the caput being at Newton Castle. The tower was damaged in a storm in 1701, and was demolished by 1791. The castle garden gave Garden Street its name.

ST JOHN'S TOWER—All that remains of the mediaeval Church of St John is this tower, located in a grassy area down Citadel Place. The tower was actually added to the ancient church in the 15th century. When the kirk was requisitioned as part of Cromwell's fort and converted to an armoury the tower was used as a watchtower. In 1853 the tower was purchased by John "Baron" Miller who added new buildings at its base and created the baronial Fort Castle. In 1914 the Marquis of Bute, a noted antiquarian and church restorer, acquired the building and restored it to its original appearance.

LOUDOUN HALL—The oldest building in Ayr, Loudoun Hall dates from around 1513, being built by James Tait, merchant in the town, and Alderman of Ayr in 1521 and from 1527-9. It gains its name from being the home of Sir Hew Campbell of Loudoun, Hereditary Sheriff of Ayr, who purchased it in 1539 as his town house. It remained in Loudoun hands until 1622. Later owned by the Bannatynes, Chalmers' and Provost John Mure, it was sold by his family in 1770 and converted into tenements, gradually degenerating into slums. From 1947-56 the building was restored by Robert Hurd for the Saltire Society.

NEWARK CASTLE—The original tower at Newark dates from the 16th century, and was built for the Kennedy family. It was extended in 1687 for James Craufurd, whose family had acquired the estate in 1601 and retained it until 1763 when it returned to Kennedy ownership. Around 1850 the tower was again extended in baronial style for the Marquis of Ailsa. Final additions in 1907-08 for Archibald Walker were designed by James Miller. Originally styled the New Wark of Bargany, the castle stands on a rock outcrop which was formerly protected by a moat.

AULD BRIG O' DOON—Celebrated in the poem "Tam o' Shanter", this magnificent single-arched bridge dates from sometime in the 15th century. The quality of the masonry is extremely fine, and it must have been a most daring construction in its day. In the poem it was here where Tam on his grey mare Meg avoided being caught by the witches who could not cross running water. According to the legend, Meg loses her tail and her hoof left a mark on a cobble, long discernible. The brig was bypassed when the New Bridge was opened in 1816 but was saved from demolition by the Revd. Hamilton Paul.

THE TOLBOOTH—The Tolbooth stood in the middle of the Sandgate and was for many years the town gaol. This old drawing shows it isolated, though in fact there were a number of buildings adjoining it, much like the "Isle" in the High Street. The tolbooth dated from 1575 though it had been altered in 1615-16 when the clock and steeple were added and again in 1754. Robert Adam produced drawings for the classicising of it in 1785, but these were not carried out. The tower was declared unsafe and demolished in 1826 to create the present wider street.

FISH CROSS—The Fish Cross was a tron, or weighing cross, which stood in the open area in front of where Marks & Spencer is now. It was erected in 1539 when the fish market and cross was built at a cost of £8 18s 2d. In 1547 it was decreed that "na kynd of stuff be sauld in tyme comyn at the fyshe cross but fysh." This illustration depicts some of the residents of Ayr in 1814 buying or selling fish. A new fishmarket was established at the harbour and in 1853 the sale of fish was banned at the cross. The cross remained in situ until around 1860, its location marked by cobbles on the roadway.

NETHER MILLS—The old mills of Ayr were established at the end of what became Mill Street, and at the foot of the Mill Brae. Weirs were erected across the River Ayr and a short sluice directed the water towards the millwheel. The mills operated for many years, and various alterations were made to the buildings in that time. In 1794 a barley mill was added and in 1795 the manufacture of snuff commenced. The mill was demolished in 1941 and the site is now a car park. The old weir survives. The rear of the County Hospital is seen behind the dam.

OVER MILLS—The site of the Over Mill of Ayr is to be seen from Overmills Bridge on the by-pass. The mill stood at the southern end of the stepping stones and operated from the 13th century. In 1761 a waulk mill was added for the fulling or beating of cloth. In 1806 the mill was altered at a cost of £531. Further improvements were made, the mill latterly having a twenty feet diameter wheel, producing thirty horsepower and driving five pairs of stones. The Over Mill was the last operating grain mill on the River Ayr, and the buildings were demolished in the spring of 1963.

THE AULD WALLACE TOWER—The present Wallace Tower stands on the site of this building, known since before 1544 as the Auld Tour. For a time owned by Robert Cathcart of Carbieston, it passed into the hands of Provost Adam Ritchie who sold it to the council in 1673. In 1731 they added the upper clock storey and belfry following a public subscription. For a time in 1749 the tower was used as a gaol. The first reference to the building as the "Wallace" Tower occurs in council minutes of 1774. The tower was recased in 1808 but was found to be unstable and subsequently demolished.

GREENAN CASTLE—The old tower of Greenan, perched precariously on its cliff-top, dates from the 16th century and stands on the site of an ancient fort. The castle was a seat of the Kennedy family. In 1602 Sir Thomas Kennedy set out for Ayr from here only to be murdered en route—the famous Auchendrane Tragedy. The tower was remodelled in 1603 for John Kennedy; the upper turrets date from that time, the wing from the late 17th century. A spiral staircase is located in the north-east corner. James Morris, who restored the Auld Brig, also did some preservation work at Greenan in 1899.

MALT CROSS—A cross of cobbles in the roadway at the junction of High Street and Sandgate marks the site of the Malt Cross. The cross was similar to the market cross of Edinburgh, having a base with column surmounted by a unicorn. It probably dated from 1697 when John Anderson, mason, was allowed to use the burgh's quarries so long as he "cast the King's armes in stoune and put the same upon the Croce of this burgh wher they ar now set upe in timber." In 1778, prior to the New Bridge being erected and New Bridge Street opened up, the cross was removed and destroyed.

AULD KIRK OF ST JOHN THE BAPTIST—When Cromwell requisitioned the old church of Ayr he granted the parishioners 1000 merks with which to build a new church. This building was erected from 1653-5 at a cost of £1733. The contractors were Theophilus Rankine, smith, John Smith, mason, and John Masoun, mason, the latter's grave is located in the kirkyard. The contract is dated 16th June 1653. T-shaped in plan, the church is a particularly fine example of 17th century Scots architecture. The Sailors' Loft contains a model of the ship "Arethusa", the other two lofts being named after the Merchants and Trades.

CROMWELL'S CITADEL—In 1652 Hans Ewald Tessin, Oliver Cromwell's engineer, designed a massive fort which was built at the mouth of the River Ayr. Six-sided, there were large bartisans at the corners and the fort covered twelve acres. Tradition states that much of the stone for the walls was brought from Ardrossan Castle. On the town side of the fort was a moat, crossed by a bridge. The original gateway through the fort walls (illustrated) survives in a lane off Citadel Place, behind Dansarena. Since the 17th century the ground level has been raised, so that today the archway is just four feet tall, though originally men on horseback could pass through. A smaller Sally Port was located at the corner of the north-western bartisan. On the wallheads were various sentry posts. Within the walls were a market place, guardhouse, storehouses, bakery, brewery, alehouse, hospital, church, smithy, stables, well, and barracks for officers, footmen, and horsemen, five hundred men in total. On the mound where Ayr Castle had stood there was a gun emplacement. The fort was abandoned by the soldiers in 1660 and the ground gifted to the Earl of Eglinton for his services to the Crown. The plan shown is one of Tessin's originals.

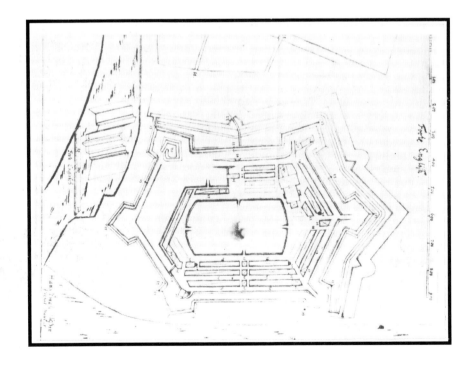

CRAIGIE HOUSE—A rather fine classical mansion, the central block of Craigie dates from around 1730 and may be the work of the architect John Smith. The house was built by Sir Thomas Wallace of Newton Castle as a replacement home, the name taken from his ancestral seat of Craigie Castle. Curved corridors lead to two wings. In 1783 ownership passed to William Campbell, whose family retained possession until 1940 when the house and grounds were bought by Ayr Town Council for £12,500. At first the house was requisitioned by the army but after 1945 it became a luxury restaurant.

TAM O' SHANTER INN—Because of its associations with Burns' poem of the same name, this old building in the High Street has been retained in its traditional appearance. Still with its thatched roof, the building was actually rebuilt in 1808 by James Shearer, though the earliest reference to it is dated 1748, when Janet Kennedy was its tenant. The burgh council bought the property in 1849 from the Shearers, but it was acquired by the Incorporation of Weavers in 1850 who retained it until 1893. The Town Council bought the inn from Andrew Turner in 1944 for £4,000, converting it to a museum in 1957.
It was in 1993 converted back into a public house.

AUCHINCRUIVE—Auchincruive House (shown above) was erected in 1767 to plans by Robert Adam for Richard Oswald. Alterations were carried out in 1830. In 1927 the estate of 665 acres was gifted to the West of Scotland Agricultural College by John M. Hannah of Girvanmains. Courses in agriculture, horticulture, food technology, poultry, engineering and mechanisation are offered by the college which was founded in Glasgow in 1899 and had been located at Holmes farm in Kilmarnock from 1904. Auchincruive House was renamed Oswald Hall, the Home Farm Gibbsyard is shown below. New buildings designed by Alex Mair were added in the 1930s and Wilson Hall designed by D.S. MacPhail was added in 1956. In recent years the college has been developing an arboretum for study purposes. The extensive and attractive grounds contain the notable Hanging Gardens which were created in the 1840s to provide employment. There is a countryside heritage centre open to the public. Across the Oswald Bridge of 1862 from the main grounds is Leglen Wood, where a cairn commemorates the wood's associations with William Wallace and Robert Burns. In 1985 a Friends of Auchincruive group was formed.

OSWALD'S TEMPLE—Known also as Auchincruive Tea House, this circular-planned building was designed by Robert Adam in his castellated style and erected in 1778 for Richard Oswald who was involved in draughting the peace treaty for the American War of Independence. The tower was based on the mausoleum of Theodoric at Ravenna. It has two floors, the lower storey containing a circular corridor with a servants room in the centre. The upper floor was where the tea would have been served. The building suffered from mining subsidence but a scheme of restoration is underway.

ROZELLE HOUSE—Robert Hamilton of Bourtreehill (Irvine) acquired these lands in 1754 and around 1755 erected Rozelle House, the name coming from one of his plantations in the West Indies. The house was enlarged in 1831, when the architect Bryce added the two wings. On 15th November 1968 Lt Commander John Hamilton gifted the house and grounds to the Burgh of Ayr as a public park and museum. The park extends to seventy acres and includes woodland walks, ponds and sculptures including Sacrifice of Christ by Ronald Rae, 1978, and Reclining Nude by Henry Moore.

FOUNDATION TABLET—When the Union Bank in the High Street (now Halifax Building Society) was erected in 1856 to the plans of Robert Paton, the workers found an old lead tablet in the foundations of the previous building to occupy the site, latterly used by the Union Bank. The tablet was placed there by John Muir, Master of the English School and Session Clerk in Ayr, and Elizabeth Chalmers, daughter of John Chalmers of Gadgirth House, which stood in Coylton Parish. The bank was later taken over by the British Linen Bank which had opened its Newmarket Street branch in 1874.

MURDOCH'S HOUSE—Formerly standing in the Sandgate, at number 58, was John Murdoch's House. This old sketch shows the thatched building prior to demolition, which took place around 1894 when the present building was erected to the plans of H.V. Eaglesham. Murdoch was the burgh schoolmaster from 1772-6, his most noted pupil being Robert Burns. The bard lived with Murdoch for three weeks in 1773 "to revise his English grammar," and to learn the basics of French. A plaque on the present building is inscribed *"Here stood the house of John Murdoch schoolmaster in which Robert Burns lodged in his 14th year and received lessons in English and French."*

SAINT QUIVOX CHURCH—The parish church of St Quivox dates from mediaeval times but was altered in 1767 for the Oswalds of Auchincruive. The parish was mentioned in a charter of 1114, spelled Sanchar, hence the Sanquhar farms nearby. The parish was joined to that of Ayr in 1895, but the church, in its kirkyard, has remained in use since then. The kirkyard contains a large mausoleum which was the burial place of the Campbells of Craigie House. It dates from 1822, being the work of the architect, W.H. Playfair. The old manse dates from 1823. In the kirkyard is an Adam and Eve stone dating from 1766. These stones are rare in Scotland, with only 45 surviving.

NEWTON OLD CHURCH—Formerly located at the end of King Street, Newton Old Church was demolished in 1963 to make way for the wide dual carriageway. There had been a campaign to save the building, which dated from 1777 and which could seat 830 worshippers, but this failed, and the church and graveyard were cleared away. The congregation had previously been united with Newton New Church in 1962. The actual kirk building was unusual in plan, having a square aisle on the south side, semi-circular apses on the other three facades. Entry to the churchyard was reached through the Newton Steeple.

WEAVER STREET—In 1751 an Act of Parliament allowed the business of weaving to be carried on outwith burghs. The trade flourished, and weavers set up their looms in their own homes. This picture shows typical weavers' housing in Newton, in the appropriately-named Weaver Street, though the street was originally known as Kilmarnock Street. The houses had two front rooms, one kept for the loom. There were about 275 looms in Ayr and district in 1776, but the American Civil War of 1861-65 prevented the importation of cotton and the trade collapsed.

NEWMARKET STREET—A short dog-leg, this street dates back to the 18th century when it was a lane known as the Trinity Vennel. In 1767 it was opened up as "the New Street" or Cross Street, but in 1814 was renamed Newmarket Street after the new butter market which was opened in it that year. MacNeille Buildings date from 1869, named after John MacNeille, Provost 1864-73. The building is decorated with the heads of John Knox, Robert the Bruce and Sir William Wallace. This photograph dates from about 1885; note the former head post office to the left.

SANDGATE HOUSE—Sandgate or Wellington House stood at the corner of what is now Boswell Park. The house dated to around 1780 and was built for John Boswell, Writer in Ayr, who died in 1805 aged 64. He was a cadet of the Auchinleck family and ancestor of the Boswells of Garrallan; his memorial is in the auld kirkyard. The house formerly had grounds around it, but in the 1890s these were laid out as Boswell Park. In 1936 the house was bought by the Post Office, demolished in 1952, and the present post office erected on the site. This view was taken from Boswell Park, the Sandgate Church can be seen to the left.

HOTEL DALBLAIR—Dalblair House was erected around 1780 in Alloway Street, though the front faced west, and an elliptical drive led off Dalblair Road. The house was owned by James Gibb, proprietor of a soap factory in the town and of Dalblair estate in the parish of Auchinleck, from where the name probably came. A later owner was David Limond, Provost from 1820-22, 1824 and 1834-41. In 1895 the house was converted to a hotel, and operated as such until 1963. Dalblair House was demolished thereafter and Dalblair Arcade shopping area built on the site in 1967.

THE FIRST "NEW" BRIDGE—From May 1786 until November 1788 a New Bridge was built across the River Ayr, linking Newton Main Street with the Sandgate, a number of buildings being demolished to allow the new access roads. The architect of this bridge is believed to be Robert Adam, although his plan may have been altered by Alexander Stevens. The bow-fronted building with the pend on the north side of the bridge was built by Stevens for himself in 1787. The bridge, which cost £4000 to build, was the one which Burns referred to, and as predicted it could not withstand one of the storms of 1877, and was partly washed away. The lower illustration is of the leaden statues which adorned the bridge abutments. Ceres is the Roman goddess of agriculture, Pan the Greek god of pastures, Marsyas the Roman god of war and Bacchvs the Greek god of wine. The statues are now located at Burns' cottage and monument. The balusters from the bridge were kept and now adorn the Pavilion forecourt. One of the armorial panels is built into the wall at the junction of Monument Road with Chapelpark Road. The chimneys to the left of the Auld Brig in the photograph are associated with the starch works and Alexander's sawmills.

CERES   PAN   MARSYAS   BACCHVS

LEADEN STATVES, FORMERLY ON THE NEW BRIDGE OF AYR — BVRNS'S BRIG

BELLEISLE HOUSE—Like Rozelle, Belleisle was named after a plantation and was erected in 1787 for Hugh Hamilton of Pinmore, nephew of Robert of Rozelle. The house was extended in 1829 by William Burn for Alexander Hamilton, converting it from Georgian to Baronial. It was later owned by William Dixon, ironmaster in Glasgow, then in 1886 by George Coats of the threadmakers. On 15th May 1926 the 290 acre estate was purchased by the burgh for £25,000 and the house converted to a hotel. The grounds were laid out as two golf courses and park, with aviary, gardens and deer park.

LIMEKILNS—This postcard depicts the old limekiln which is passed by the River Ayr Walk. The three-draw kiln was used to burn limestone and convert it to lime which was in big demand at one time both to reduce the acid content of soil, thus improving farmland, and in the manufacture of iron. There used to be a number of limekilns within Ayr, one of them giving the name to Limekiln Road in Newton. There were limekilns on both sides of the harbour (the one on the south side being erected in 1787), off Alloway Street, and the other located approximately where Elba Street is today.

AYR BARRACKS—Taken within the courtyard of the infantry barracks, this photograph (above) shows the main block of the soldiers' quarters. In 1794 the former Sugar House at the harbour was converted for military use and the camp was formed. This was closed in 1815 when the war with France ended. In 1820 the barracks were reopened, the 10th Hussars and 4th Royal Veteran Battalion being stationed there. The garrison was rebuilt in 1873 following a fire in the Sugar House, and was the nominated headquarters of the Royal North British Fusiliers, Ayrshire's county regiment, renamed the Royal Scots Fusiliers in 1881. The barracks were renamed the Churchill Barracks in 1942 after the great Prime Minister. The lower photograph shows the Prince of Wales inspecting the 4th/5th Royal Scots Fusiliers Territorial Battalion. With him is Col. M.B. Buchanan, Commanding Officer of the regiment. The R.S.F. amalgamated with the Highland Light Infantry in 1959 to create the Royal Highland Fusiliers. The barracks were closed that year and the R.H.F. moved to Redford Barracks in Edinburgh.

NEWTON CROSS—The market cross of the Burgh of Newton of Ayr is inscribed "Newtoun 1675 Rebuilt 1775" at the top, though this is badly eroded. The cross was originally located adjacent to Newton Tolbooth (seen on the left of the sketch below). It stood for a time in Newton kirkyard, but was later moved to the present site at the north end of the New Bridge, Robert Cuthbert paying for its reconstruction. The cross has occupied a few sites hereabouts, however, previously being located further east. The base is modern.

NEWTON TOLBOOTH—The tolbooth or steeple at Newton was erected in 1795, which date appears on the four clock faces. It contains a bell by Mears, dated 1795. This drawing by Robert Bryden, depicting Main Street in 1825, shows the tolbooth in its original setting, with the Newton Cross in front, Newton Kirk behind, and the old mill lade running down the middle of the street. The building was formerly surrounded by the burgh's Assembly Rooms, or council offices, and access to Newton Kirk (the gable to the right) could be made through the archway. The Assembly Room replaced the old Newton Tolbooth which had been erected in 1647 by the Freemen of Newton. The other photograph, taken from the Orient Cinema, shows how the tower was left isolated in 1963 when King Street was widened. The remaining tower was restored in 1968. Newton New Church is seen to the left.

OLD RACECOURSE—Horse racing has taken place in Ayr for many years, originally along the shore. The old racecourse to the south of the town was given by Royal Charter to the burgh in the 14th century as a common. In 1770 it was laid out as a racecourse and the earliest recorded race to take place was in October 1775 when a prize of £50 was offered. In 1787 the first "viewhouse" was put up to improve the spectators' view of the racing – this was extended in 1817. An enclosing dike was erected in 1788. In 1791 the course was leased from the council by the race committee. In 1808 the first race for the Ayr Gold Cup was run, and in 1824 the first Western Meeting. In 1907 the course was closed when the new racecourse was opened. The ground, which extends to around 64 acres, was then converted to playing fields and partially for Seafield golf course. The upper picture shows the racecourse whilst it was still in use, the two large houses to the back being Shalimar and Hartley House. The lower photograph is of the former stand on a race meet. One of the racecourse buildings erected in 1867 was converted to a pavilion for the playing fields when the course was closed. It was later rebuilt as View House.

MACADAM'S MEMORIAL—John Loudoun MacAdam is thought to have been born in Ayr in 1756, in Lady Cathcart's House in the Sandgate, though other accounts put his place of birth at Carsphairn. He invented a method of preparing a road surface using graded stones which was known as "Macadamising" - the tar was not added until later. MacAdam died in 1836 and was buried at Moffat. This memorial was erected by the Institution of Municipal and County Engineers in Wellington Square on the centenary of his death, the photograph showing the unveiling.

MORAVIAN CHURCH—The Moravian Brethren were episcopalian in their beliefs. The first Moravians were converted in Ayr in 1765, forming a Moravian Society. By 1778 there were sufficient numbers to erect a little church behind the houses of Mill Street – reached through an entrance doorway. There were almost 200 members in 1836. The church, shown in this sketch of 1887, was a simple building, with school room upstairs (opened in 1816) and graveyard to the rear. The manse was formerly attached, but latterly was located at 2 Cassillis Street. The church closed in 1916.

CASTLEHILL HOUSE—Patrick Ballantine erected Castlehill in 1804 on the site of an older mansion. In 1810 the house passed to his brother, lawyer, banker and former provost John Ballantine, who had held office in 1787-89, 1793-95 and 1796-98. It was to John Ballantine that Burns dedicated his poem, "The Brigs of Ayr", Ballantine being responsible for the design of the new bridge, getting the plans from Adam whilst in London. The house remained in Ballantine hands until 1909. In the 1960s the house was demolished to make way for the new general hospital which was proposed for the site – but this was later built near the Ailsa.

CONTENT HOUSE—The Fire Station now occupies the site of this small country house. The house may have been a traditional Ayrshire farmhouse which was extended, with the addition of a large Venetian window and pediment on the south-east front. At one time owned by the MacIlwraiths, John (1778-1853) owning a copperworks, his sons John (1832-1902) and Sir Thomas (1835-1900) founding a large shipping company. Sir Thomas was three times Premier of Queensland. This painting shows the house's principal south-eastern front, distinguished by the window. Content House was demolished in 1961.

WELLINGTON SQUARE—The square was laid out in 1806 or thereabouts, the first building being Wellington House (Number 25) which was erected that year by Provost Charles Shaw. Most of the other buildings date from between 1810 and 1820. The original intention had been to build on the central area. This view, taken from the roof of the buildings at the east end, shows the square earlier this century. In the centre is the cenotaph, towards the courthouse the statue of Lord Eglinton. The Pavilion can be seen to the left of the Sheriff Court House which is prominent at the top of the picture. The Sheriff Court dates from 1818-22 and was built to the plans of Robert Wallace. The building, which comprised a court, hall and prison to the rear, cost £30,000 and was paid for by the burgh council in collaboration with the Commissioners of Supply. The Justiciary Court Room could accommodate 600 people. The county hall has since been converted for court use.

NEW CHURCH—The New Church, though it dates from 1807-10, was so-called from its foundation as an extension to the Auld Kirk, which could not cope with its members. Located in Fort Street, it was designed by David Hamilton. The building cost £6000 and had seating for 880 worshippers. A pipe organ was installed in 1874 and alterations made in 1900. The church was in 1951 renamed the Cathcart Church when it was amalgamated with Cathcart Street Church. In 1981 the New Church congregation joined with the Auld Kirk and the building was converted to a dance school, named Dansarena, in 1984.

COUNTY GAOL—The gaol was opened in 1822, financed jointly by Ayr Burgh Council and the Commissioners of Supply for Ayrshire. Robert Wallace was the architect responsible for the design. The upper photograph shows the gaol from the south, with the Sheriff Court to the right. The gaol was known among the prisoners as their "cottage by the sea" - to locals it provided cheap carpet cleaning services. The former Debtor's Wing was later converted to a prison for female prisoners. The inmates were kept hard at labour for fourteen hours per day, from six in the morning until eight at night. They were kept apart from each other, even at meal times. The prison accommodated an average of eighteen convicts per day in 1837. The gaol was demolished in 1931, as shown in the lower photograph. Note the use of horses and carts for removing the rubble. The County Buildings now occupy the site.

BURNS' MONUMENT—The Burns' Monument at Alloway owes its origin to Sir Alexander Boswell, son of the more famous James Boswell. He called a public meeting, at which only he and his manservant attended, to raise a memorial to Burns. Nevertheless, the fund went ahead and soon managed to raise the £3,300 required. David Hamilton designed the memorial, waiving his fee. The foundation stone was laid by Boswell on 25th January 1820, the monument opened on 23rd July 1823. The triangular base was to represent Kyle, Carrick and Cunninghame, with nine columns above, rising to sixty feet.

BURNS' MONUMENT HOTEL—Erected in 1829, the Burns Monument Hotel was originally named the Burns Arms Inn and was operated by James Begbie. The New Statistical Account, written in 1837, commended Mr Auld for embellishing the gardens and enhancing the natural beauties of the location. The architect Allan Stevenson designed alterations to the building in 1903-04. Behind the hotel, between the two brigs of Doon, are the famous tea gardens, in great demand for wedding photographs. Also within the gardens is a sculptured head, which may be by local artist James Thom.

ST MARGARET'S CHAPEL—The Roman Catholic church of St Margaret in John Street was erected in 1826 to the plans of James Dempster, and was described as "the handsomest church in Ayr". Gothic in style, the church had an adjoining school which was closed when St Margarets School in Whitletts Road was extended. To the rear of the chapel, reached from Content Street, is a burial ground. The first priest, William Thomson, had to serve the Catholics from all over Ayrshire until a second was appointed in 1845. He died in 1859. In 1893 the transepts and apsed sanctuary were added by the architect D. Sturrock.

WALLACETOWN PARISH CHURCH—Wallacetown Parish Church was erected in 1834 by public subscription as a chapel-of-ease for St Quivox parishioners, but was granted a district of its own in 1836. The architect was John Kay who used the Tudoresque style. The church received full status on 9th March 1874. The hall was opened in 1936 to mark the kirk's centenary. The twin towers at the front were lowered in height at the renovations of 1948-52, the church being rededicated on 16th December 1952. Adjoining the church was a school, now converted to halls.

WALLACE TOWER—Built in 1834 to the plans of Thomas Hamilton, the Wallace Tower was erected on the site of a previous building, also known as the Wallace Tower (see p34) though there seems to be no connection with either Sir William Wallace nor the Wallaces of Craigie. There had been two previous attempts to replace the original tower. In 1808 the old tower was resurfaced with new stone but the original foundations had been inadequate and it was decided to demolish the building completely. A new tower was erected by 1831, but there was a serious flaw in it and it collapsed. The present tower, standing 113 feet high in four storeys and costing £2200 to build, has a statue of the great patriot on the southern side, sculpted by the local artist, James Thom of Tarbolton (1799-1850), and paid for by public subscription. The tower contains two bells, one cast in France and dated 1639, relocated from the original tower, the other made for the tower and dated 1834. These were originally used to chime out the hours. In 1929 there was a proposal to re-erect the tower on another site, to aid traffic flow, but this came to nought. Instead, the ground floor was opened up to allow pedestrians to pass through.

TOWN HALL—The Municipal Buildings on the corner of High Street and Sandgate were erected from 1827-32 to the plans of Thomas Hamilton. Classical in style, Hamilton produced a magnificent steeple 217 feet in height, damaged in 1836 when it was struck by lightning. A few large blocks were thrown to the ground, but did not cause any real damage. The town hall cost £10,000 to erect. In 1878-81 the buildings were extended to the High Street to the plans of Campbell Douglas and Sellars, as shown in the sketch of that time. The building was damaged by a fire in 1897 and the interiors were rebuilt by J.K. Hunter.

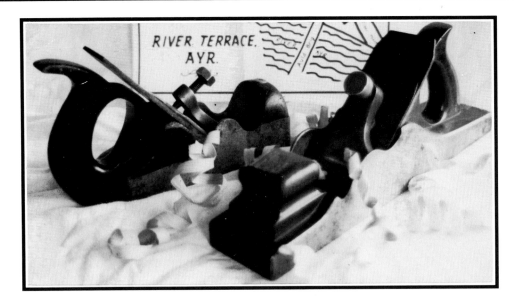

SPIERS PLANES—The factory of Stewart Spiers was located across the Auld Brig in River Terrace. He was one of six sons who was apprenticed to the family cabinetmaking business, but he commenced plane manufacture in 1840, exhibiting them at the Great Exhibition of 1851. Spiers made woodworking planes of the highest quality, perhaps introducing the rosewood infil to the dovetailed sole and sides; certainly his method was copied by many other makers, including Norris of London and Mathieson of Glasgow. Spiers made planes until the introduction of the American-style Stanley planes became the norm in the 20th century.

THE FIRST RAILWAY STATION—The original railway station in Ayr was located at Newton, access being made from Darlington Place. This sketch shows the official opening of the Glasgow and Ayr Railway on 11th August 1840, looking south to the town steeple. The station remained in passenger use until 1857 when it was converted to a goods station, known as Ayr Goods or Ayr North Side. A number of sidings were constructed and lines continued on to the north and south harbour quays. The station continued to operate until around 1956. The site has now been redeveloped with factory units, houses and shops.

LIGHTHOUSE—The harbour lighthouse, which originally displayed a fixed white light, now flashing green, dates from 1841-3 and was designed by Robert Paton. Rising five storeys in height, it has a corbelled parapet. A second light (flashing red) is located next to the Pilot House. When these are in line the correct course to enter the harbour is being taken. A small light-keeper's cottage was built alongside about 1850. The lighthouse and cottage were acquired by the Scottish Maritime Museum in 1986 and restoration work followed.

FEVER HOSPITAL—The Fever Hospital, an attractive three-storey building, stood at the junction of Smith and Mill streets, set back from the road in a sizeable garden. Erected between 1841-4, and run by a committee, it had twenty beds at the beginning but had to cope with more cases with the outbreak of cholera. In 1875 it was converted to a general hospital, known as the Ayr Hospital. It was soon found to be too small and was replaced by Ayr County. The building was demolished and the present tenements at the corner of Smith Street erected in the grounds.

LADY JANE HAMILTON'S SCHOOL—Lady Jane Hamilton's School in Charlotte Street operated from 1843 until 1936, and was initially a charity school. It was financed by Archibald Hamilton of Rozelle and named after his wife, Lady Jane Montgomerie, daughter of the Earl of Eglinton. The school was taken over by the school board in 1872 and the building, originally T-shaped in plan, extended thereafter. This photograph, taken around 1911, shows the teachers in the school. From left to right they are- Back row: Miss Hardwick, Miss Clarke, Miss Fullarton, Miss Cameron and Miss Miller. Front Row: Miss Edgar, Miss Graham (the headmistress) and Miss MacKay.

SANDGATE CHURCH—Erected in 1845, this church was the outcome locally of the national Disruption of 1843, when many ministers and members left the Church of Scotland in a row over patronage. The Ayr Free Church was built in 1845 to plans by William Gale. In the intervening years they had worshipped in a wooden building at Alloway Place. The first minister was Revd William Grant, formerly of Wallacetown Parish Church. A hall was added in 1878, facing Fort Street. At the Union in 1929 it became the Sandgate Church of Scotland but in 1981 the building was closed, and later converted to a saleroom.

JOHN TAYLOR'S STATUE—John Taylor was born on 16th September 1805 at Newark Castle. He lived at Blackhouse, a small mansion which stood where Western House is now. He stood unsuccessfully for Ayr Burghs in 1832. Taylor was a follower of the Chartists and was sent to prison for his radical beliefs, having printed libellous articles in the "Ayrshire Reformer" which he edited. He was arrested in July 1839 for inciting a riot in Birmingham but was released in August. His health suffered thereafter and he died on 4th December 1842 at Larne. This memorial statue was erected in Wallacetown Cemetery in 1850.

CAMBUSDOON HOUSE—James Baird (1802-76) was born at Old Monkland. He owned the Gartsherrie ironworks at Coatbridge, and in 1844 purchased the Eglinton ironworks at Kilwinning. By 1869 Baird's owned 26 of the 48 blast furnaces in the county. He bought the Greenfield estate at Alloway and there erected Cambusdoon in 1853. He bought other estates in the county over the years, Auchendrane in 1862, Muirkirk (1863), Drumellan (1866) and Wellwood (1873), totalling 20,000 acres. He gifted thousands of pounds to charity, building the town's dry dock, and Alloway Church, where he is buried. He gifted £500,000 to the Church of Scotland, and the Baird Trust is still used for religious development.

BARON MILLER AND FORT CASTLE—John Watson Miller was brought up at Catrine and was a nephew of one of Burns' "Mauchline Belles". He was apprenticed to Mr MacCririck in Ayr as a gunsmith before moving to Bengal where he continued to make guns, making himself a reasonable fortune in business in Calcutta. In 1853 he purchased the Fort area of the town from the Kennedys, which had in 1663 been created the Barony of Montgomeriestoun, hence his right to style himself Baron Miller. The Burgh of Ayr had hoped to buy this ground, but failed to win it at auction. An antiquarian, Miller was also something of an eccentric, building himself a castle out of St John's Tower. The architect for this was John Murdoch, whose practice was in Ayr. At one of the corners of the citadel walls Miller erected a curiously corbelled sentinel post by his own hands, used as a garden gazebo, but known as Miller's Folly, seen in the photograph above. He was also skilled at making fiddles. John Miller died at Fort Castle on 21st June 1910 in his ninetieth year. By then most of his lands had been developed, leaving only the ground around the tower. Miller offered to sell this ground to the Burgh as a park, but they refused.

AYR FREE CHURCH—Long known as the Martyrs' Church, this fine old building dates from 1832. It was built by the Reformed Presbyterians who followed the Covenanting, Bible-adhering tradition. The congregation still sing unaccompanied from the Scottish Psalter. In 1876 the church united with the Free Church, but in 1900 many refused to join the United Free Church. The Free congregation met for a time in the Wallace Tower until in 1907 the Royal Commissioners allocated this building to the Free Church continuing, now the second oldest church still in use in Ayr. A hall was added in 1992-93.

AYR RAILWAY STATION—Townhead Station was opened on 7th August 1856, when the new line to Dalmellington was inaugurated. The station was on 1st July 1857 designated the passenger station for Ayr, the old station used for goods only thereafter. A number of sidings existed on the west side of the station, which has four platforms. In 1886 the station was rebuilt, the great hotel building being added, designed by Andrew Galloway, chief engineer with G.S.W.R. The cost of the hotel was £50,000. The railway was electrified in 1987 with the new name of "Ayrline".

KYLE COMBINATION POORHOUSE—The poorhouse in Holmston Road was erected 1857-60 to the plans of William Lambie Moffat. It replaced an older poorhouse of 1755 which stood in Mill Street opposite Smith Street and was demolished in 1921. The Kyle Combination Poorhouse was operated by eight parish councils and had accommodation for 150 poor. The building is now known as Holmston House, offices of the Social Work department. The Governor's House stands adjacent, as does one original gatehouse.

CHARLOTTE STREET POLICE STATION—Now the offices of the council water department, this building in Charlotte Street was erected in 1858 as the County Constabulary headquarters. The Burgh Constabulary was formed in 1850 with Donald MacDonald as Superintendent of eight constables. The Burgh and County constabularies remained separate until 1968. Prior to 1850 there had just been men appointed as constables on an annual basis and the locals enforcing the law known as the "Black Gang". The station was closed in 1975 when the new station was opened in King Street.

ALLOWAY PARISH CHURCH—Erected in 1858, Alloway church was designed by Campbell Douglas. Costing £1750 to erect, the belfry stands 66 feet in height. Gothic in style, it has stained glass windows by Stephen Adam, C.W. Whall, Clayton & Bell, W & J Kier, Guthrie & Wells and Douglas MacLundie. On 4th July 1860 Alloway was made a Quoad Sacra parish, the first minister, Revd. John Lochhead between. The church was extended in 1889-91 by MacVicar Anderson. The modern church hall was added in 1964 to plans of Cowie & Torry. A small kirkyard is located to the rear of the church.

DARLINGTON PLACE CHURCH—This church, which had 800 seats, was erected as a United Presbyterian place of worship in 1860 to the plans of Clarke & Bell. The congregation had moved from the old church which stood in a lane behind Wallace Street, the site now occupied by Asda. The church hall was located in River Street. From 1948 until the church was closed in 1981 it was known as Darlington New Church. In 1986-88 the building was converted to a workshop for the Borderline Theatre Company. This photograph was taken in September 1860 and shows the church between the Foresters Arms and the Toll at the bridge end.

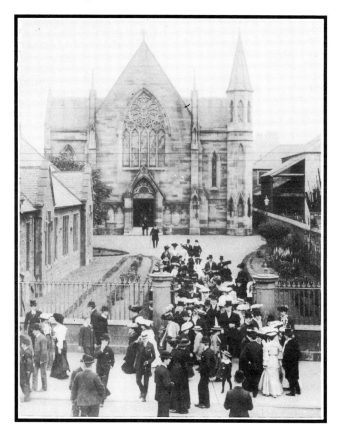

NEWTON NEW CHURCH—The Newton New Church originated at the Disruption of 1843 when Revd James Stevenson and most of his congregation left the parish church and formed their own Free Church. A church was erected in 1844, but this was demolished and the church shown erected in 1862 to the plans of William Clarke, having 900 seats. On the left is the church hall of 1791, replaced by halls of 1971. The congregation rejoined the Church of Scotland in 1929, becoming known as Newton New Church, but in 1962 the two Newton congregations were united in this building, thereafter known as Newton Parish Church.

PRIMROSE KENNEDY'S FOUNTAIN—Originally located at the junction of the Sandgate with Fort Street, this pink granite fountain was erected by subscription in 1868 in honour of Primrose William Kennedy (1800-63), being unveiled on 11th August. It was constructed of Aberdeen granite by Andrew Hunter, builder, Ayr. Kennedy was a noted banker in the county, and acted as Provost of Ayr from 1855-61. Kennedy was a member of the Western Bank, but in 1855 became agent for the Royal Bank when its new premises were opened at the corner of Newmarket Street and the Sandgate. He lived at Drumellan House which is near Maybole. In 1993 the monument was relocated in Wellington Square. The photograph shows the fountain being removed from Fort Street prior to its re-erection in Wellington Square.

JAMES NEILL'S STATUE—Standing in Wellington Square, the statue to General James George Smith Neill was sculpted by Matthew Noble and erected in 1859. Neill was born in Wellington Square in 1810, son of Colonel Neill of Barnweill and Swindridgemuir. He obtained a cadetship in the East India Company in 1827 and swiftly climbed through the ranks to become Brigadier-General. Neill was active at Cawnpore during the Indian Mutiny. He was shot at the relief of Lucknow in India on 25th September 1857. There are other memorials to Neill in India and his grave can be seen in the Auld Kirkyard.

GARTFERRY HOUSE—Built in 1867, to the plans of Andrew MacLachlan, Gartferry House was originally the home of Robert Paton. Located at 44 Racecourse Road, the building was later owned by Charles D. Cree followed by Miss Esther Barclay. Italianate in style, the house stands in one third of an acre of grounds. In 1930 Gartferry was converted to a hotel by Fairbairns of Glasgow. In the stone wall surrounding the grounds can still be found the three stones which formerly supported the gibbet on the Over Tolbooth.

SEATOWER—A tall castle-like building, Seatower was erected in Racecourse Road around 1860. The architect may have been David MacGibbon, whose work it resembles. The house was built for David Hunter (whose initials appear on the staircase window), but was later owned by Colonel William Parker Adam (died 1910) followed by Robert Parker Adam then John Gray. The house was afterwards converted to a hotel. In 1977 the building was extended and a modern block was added to the west and the whole was converted to flats.

WALLACE ALLAN'S—Wallace Allan's jewellery and watchmaking business was established in 1873. At the end of the 19th century he acquired these premises at the junction of Newmarket and Hope streets. Allan was a councillor in the town for a time. In the 1920s he made a copy of the Eiffel Tower, at that time used as a transmitter for timechecks, and arranged for a ball in it to fall when these signals were made. The shop was at one time noted for its public barometer, but this was removed in 1980. The boy standing at the door is Robert Allan, elder son of the founder.

MATTHEW MARK & SON—Matthew Mark was born in Germany in 1832. He was a clockmaker to trade and emigrated to Ayr in 1859. He later became a British citizen. Mark found work by winding up the clocks in local mansions, but in 1863 he set up his own clockmaker's and jewellery business at 11 Newmarket Street, in which shop the business continues. It remained in Mark family ownership until 1969, being bought by Brian Martin in 1972. This photograph shows the original Matthew Mark at the shop door. The facade has remained virtually unaltered from that day to this.

AILSA HOSPITAL—The Ailsa Hospital, or Glengall Asylum as it was originally known, was erected between 1865-68 to care for mentally handicapped patients. The hospital was extended in 1891 to accommodate 355 persons. The hospital was transferred to the Western Regional Hospitals Board on 5th July 1948, along with other hospitals in the area. There are a number of separate blocks in the wooded grounds. This view shows the bowling green.

EARL OF EGLINTON'S STATUE—Erected in 1865 to the memory of Archibald, 13th Earl of Eglinton and Winton, this statue was sculpted by Matthew Noble. Lord Eglinton was born in 1812 and succeeded to the title in 1819. In 1839 he was responsible for the famous Eglinton Tournament at Eglinton Castle which was a financial disaster due to the poor weather. The "Tournament" was to consist of mounted knights in shining armour, jousting in the lists – spectators came from all over the country and the starting parade consisted of 2 military bands, more than 100 mounted men, well over 100 armed retainers on foot, The Duke of Atholl with a company of his Atholl Highlanders, the thirteen competing knights and their retinues and much more besides. The cost of the event to the Earl was said to have been £40,000. Nevertheless, he continued his love of horse-racing, one of his horses winning the Derby in 1849. He became the Lord Lieutenant of Ayrshire and Viceroy of Ireland He died on 4th October 1861.

WELLINGTON SCHOOL—This private school for girls was established in 1839, at first located at 22 Wellington Square, hence the name. The founder was Mrs Gross whose husband, Solomon Gross, had been a languages teacher at the Academy. Twenty "young ladies of quality" boarded at the school and were taught elocution, embroidery, history, French and the piano. Carleton Turrets in Craigweil Road was acquired in 1923 and converted to a new base for the school. For a time boys were also taught, at Hartfield House and Hartree House. Westfield and Sleaford houses were also added to the Wellington School complex. From September 1994 the school became co-educational, with first intake of boys bringing the roll up to 520.

BOYS' INDUSTRIAL SCHOOL—The Boys' School of Industry was erected at Commonhead in St Leonard's Road in 1874 to the plans of John Murdoch. In 1891 it had 93 boys in attendance. A Girls' School of Industry was added in 1896, located in Belmont Avenue (designed by James Morris), latterly used as St Leonard's Special School. That building is now demolished and replaced by Rosebank School. The Boys' Industrial School was later converted to the Technical College, then Ayr Training Workshops, but is currently empty.

THE NEW BRIDGE—Dating from 1877-79 (the year 1878 is inscribed on the parapet), the New Bridge was built to replace the earlier New Bridge of 1787, which Burns had predicted would become a "shapeless cairn" and be outlived by the Auld Brig. Costing £15,000 to build, the bridge was designed by the engineers Blyth and Cunningham. It has five arches and is built of sandstone, the parapet of white granite supporting cast iron lamps. The lower photograph was taken in 1878 and shows the early stages of construction. The timber supporting frames for the arches are in place on the southern two arches, and some voussoirs have been laid. The Auld Brig, which temporarily had a new lease of life, is seen to the rear. The New Bridge marks approximately the upper limit of the port of Ayr. The exact position is marked on the walls of North and South Harbour streets where two square white marble stones are inscribed "AB", for Ayr Burgh.

EXCAVATION OF NEW DOCK—In 1878 the Wet Dock on the Newton side of the harbour was excavated from the solid rock. This photograph shows work underway. Extending to eight acres, financial assistance for the project was given by James Baird of Cambusdoon. The docks were surrounded by numerous railway sidings. As early as 1775, when A. & M. Armstrong printed their map of Ayr, there is reference to "Newton Loch, proposed for a dry dock". This location is now occupied by Green Street.

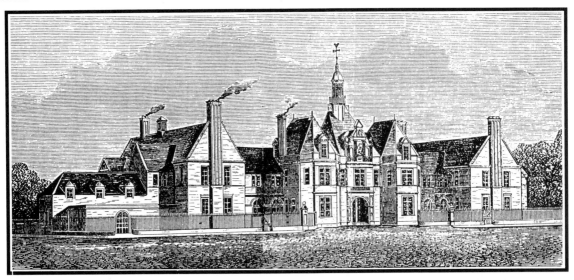

AYR COUNTY HOSPITAL—The hospital in Holmston Road was erected 1881-3 to the plans of John Murdoch at a cost of £11,500 including furnishings and equipment. Over the entrance is a carving depicting the Good Samaritan. Forty-four patients could be accommodated in the general hospital (24 male, 16 female and 4 children) plus another twenty in the fever ward. The wards were named afer local estates or landowners. The official opening on 13th February 1883 was performed by R.F.F. Campbell of Craigie. The hospital was closed on 31st October 1991.

AYR SHIPYARD—The shipyard in Ayr was established in 1883 by Samuel MacKnight & Company, but boatbuilding had taken place in Ayr on a smaller scale previously. The new yard was located at the west end of the south quay, a long slip built on a north-south axis down which ships were launched. The slip was crossable on foot by a swing bridge. Boats built by MacKnight included the "Madge Wildfire", a 210 ton passenger steamer launched on 17th June 1886, the "Lady Rowena", a 332 ton vessel of 1891, and the "Britannia", launched in 1896. This latter ship was bought by Campbell & Co., who also had the "Westward Ho!" built at Ayr. In 1902 the yard was taken over by the Ailsa Shipbuilding Company to build paddle steamers and coasters. The "Ailsa" was made in 1924, a small 120 ton ship which plied from Girvan to the Ailsa Craig until 1932. Taken from the South Pier, this photograph shows the shipyard of Ayr with its many cranes. The tower on the left was used by the coastguard as a lookout. The lower photograph shows the launching of the "Ville de Papeete" in 1928, the second last ship to be built at Ayr, ordered by a French company. The yard closed during the winter of 1928-29, but was opened temporarily during the Second World War.

SAVOY PARK—Now known as the Savoy Park Hotel, this large house was erected in Racecourse Road between 1884-86 when it was called Red House. The architect was James Morris. It was extended in 1898 and again in 1906-9. The house was built for Charles Lindsay Orr Ewing (1860-1903), who was elected as Member of Parliament for Ayr Burghs in 1895 and 1900. He was the fifth son of Sir Archibald Orr Ewing, Baronet. Savoy Park was later converted for hotel use. William C. Henderson took over in 1960. The Ayr County Club held its meetings here after leaving the building which became Queen's Court.

WOODEN KIRK MISSION—In 1881 a mission of the Ayrshire Christian Union was set up in Wallacetown which held its meetings in a timber hut, hence its nickname, the Wooden Kirk Mission. In time this name became recognised, especially in October 1898 when a new brick-built hall was opened in Limond's Wynd, to the plans of William MacClelland. The large hall could seat 221, the smaller hall 94, but when the connecting doors were opened a greater congregation could be seated. In 1951 a new mission was formed in the church, sponsored by Newton Old Church. The Wooden Kirk was demolished in January 1968.

NEWTON TOWN DRUMMER—This picture shows the old town drummer of Newton-upon-Ayr. Town drummers were common in olden days to read proclamations and make other public announcements. On the ground stands a hand bell. These were similarly common in attracting attention prior to announcements, and also for ringing at the front of a funeral cortege. A bell-ringer would be paid a penny a mile on such occasions, walking from the deceased's home to the kirkyard. Ayr had its own drummer, but when Matthew Bellamy died in 1888 he was not replaced.

AYRSHIRE VOLUNTEER REGIMENT—Taken at the Harbour Street entrance to Ayr barracks, this picture shows the members of the 1/1 Battalion of the Ayrshire Volunteer Regiment. The group's headquarters was in the barracks. The regiment was founded in 1860 as an infantry equivalent to the Ayrshire Yeomanry Cavalry, itself founded in 1798. In 1887 the Volunteer Regiment was formed into a voluntary battalion of the Royals Scots Fusiliers.

ANDREW LEES & SONS—Shoemaking was once a major source of employment in Ayr. This photograph shows the St Crispin's Works of Andrew Lees which was located at 6-8 McCall's Avenue, built in 1901 to plans by Allan Stevenson. Note the overhead driveshafts which are connected to the stitching machinery by belts and the various sizes of pre-cut leather soles in the boxes. Andrew Lees (1859-1934) was a member of the Maybole shoemaking family. The factory was taken over by Harry Beebee in 1966 but is now closed down.

THE BACK O' THE ISLE—Now known as Hope Street, previously the narrow thoroughfare from the Fish Cross past Newmarket Street was called the Back o' the Isle. This old photograph shows it at the turn of the century, with Wallace Allan's jewellery shop to the right (earlier the Wallace Tavern), Hugh MacKenzie's to the left. Next down Hope Street is John Lochhead's Sale Rooms, a bakery, John Paterson's leather merchants, and James Gebbie's shoe-shop, with the gable bearing the "Sporting Chronicle" sign.

CATTLE MARKET—Operated by James Craig & Son, as is the abattoir at Heathfield, the cattle market in Ayr was established in 1205 when William the Lion granted the burgh charter. The sale of cattle originally took place at the Fauldbacks, the ground behind the gardens at the end of Alloway Street. Following the creation of Burns Statue Square and the station, the market moved to Castlehill Road (shown) in 1891. James Craig commenced his trade as an auctioneer in 1889. In 1993 plans were passed to allow the erection of a supermarket on the market site, this being relocated at Whitefordhill.

SAVOY CROFT AND JAMES MORRIS—James Morris (1857-1942), one of the finest architects in Ayr, built Savoy Croft as his home in 1892-93, extending it in 1914. The house has a very fine Arts and Crafts interior and remained in Morris hands until 1991. Morris trained as an architect with Lindsay Miller in Glasgow before setting up in Ayr with James Hunter. He was responsible for saving the Auld Brig, for donating a coat of arms to Ayr Academy in 1912 and for founding the Scottish Society of Art Workers. Morris wrote a number of books, *A Romance of Industrial Engineering* being a history of Glenfield & Kennedy, the *Auld Toon o' Ayr* in 1928 and *Ayrshire White Needlework* in 1916.

STEVEN FOUNTAIN—The Steven Fountain was presented to the town by James Steven, ironfounder in Glasgow, who resided for a time at Skeldon House near Dalrymple. He died on 8th February 1903. The fountain was unveiled and the water was turned on in September 1892. Made of cast iron, it is decorated with dolphins and an otter with a fish. The fountain was refurbished by Kyle and Carrick District Council to mark the naming of Place de Saint-Germain-en-Laye by M. le Maire Michel Pericard on 6th June 1987.

POST OFFICE-The sandstone baronial post office in the Sandgate was opened for business in 1893. Previously the post office had bee located in Newmarket Street in 1872. The Sandgate office was designed by Walter Robertson of the Board of Works for Scotland. The building was extended in 1907 to the plans of W.T. Oldrieve. When the Post Office moved to new premises in 1952 the old building was converted to the Registrar's Office.

Note the cobbled street in the photograph. The present Post Office was opened in 1968.

CARNEGIE LIBRARY—Andrew Carnegie, the wealthy ironmaster, gifted £10,000 for the erection of a free library in Ayr. This building, designed by Campbell Douglas and Morrison, was opened on 2nd September 1893. On the stairway is a stained glass window by Stephen Adam of Glasgow which depicts Carnegie as well as a figure of a woman representing Knowledge, bearing six toes on one of her feet! In 1934 a new reference room was added. In addition to a lending collection, the library contains a reference department, exhibition area, and many early records concerning the burgh of Ayr.

ST ANDREW'S CHURCH—Located in Park Circus, St Andrew's church is distinguished by its 150 feet tall red sandstone spire. Gothic Perpendicular in style, the designer was John Bennie Wilson, winner of an architectural competition. The church was erected in 1893 for the Free congregation which had separated from Wallacetown Free Church in 1889, meeting during the intervening years in the Artillery Hall in Newmarket Street. A hall was added to the church in 1897 to the plans of William MacClelland. The church became a United Free church in 1900 and Church of Scotland at the Union of 1929.

ALLOWAY—The little village of Alloway lay quite dormant from the time the church was abandoned until around the 18th century. Burns' father was one of a few who built a house in the little street, and gradually the community started its next spell of life. William Burnes built the road known as Greenfield Avenue in 1756, and this may have been the stimulus to growth. After a number of years there were established a smithy and a post office. Following the death of Burns and the erection of his memorial, visitors came to the village to see his birthplace, for many years converted to an inn. In 1849 a school was built at the junction of Doonholm Road to serve the district, but as the village grew despite being enlarged it became too small. In 1895 the Public School at Alloway was built, at which time James Turnbull was the schoolmaster. The flagpole in front of the school was erected in memory of John Hutchison of Newarkhill in 1905. The former school was in 1896 converted to a public hall and in 1929 the architect Robert Lorimer was commissioned to carry out various alterations. An exterior wall carries a memorial to the Alloway victims of the great wars.

DANIEL MAIN, FOR 50 YEARS COXSWAIN
AYR LIFEBOAT. DIED 1895.
AGED 69·

LIFEBOAT STATION—The lifeboat station in Ayr commenced in 1803 and in the following year a grant from Lloyd's Society enabled a ten-oared boat to be bought. This was gifted to the Harbour Trust and used in many rescues. In 1819 a replacement boat was acquired and it was on it Daniel Main served. He had the honour of being coxswain of Ayr lifeboat for over fifty years, dying in 1895 aged 69. In 1859 the Royal National Life Boat Institution (later RNLI) made its first local donation. In 1867 a new boat was launched at Ayr, the "Janet Hoyle", paid for by Thomas Hardie of London and named in honour of his wife. The lower photograph shows another "Janet Hoyle" at its launch on 11th June 1910 performed by the Countess of Glasgow. This boat required twelve oarsmen, was 35 feet in length and cost £1007 1s 8d. On the 27th December 1930 the Ayr lifeboat was called out to render assistance. The station in Ayr was closed in 1932, the buildings at the foot of Fort Street being in recent years converted to a restaurant.

DOONFOOT MILL—This early photograph depicts the Doonfoot Mill, which formerly ground corn and flour. Tradition states that Burns composed "The Banks of Doon" here. The weir was damaged by ice in 1896 but was rebuilt. The mill was acquired by the Greenan Laundry Company Limited in 1896 and considerably extended. The laundry was operated by Messrs. Bowie of Ayr. The chimney, which stood 100 feet tall, and the laundry were demolished in 1971.

AYR OBSERVER PRINTING WORKS—The "Ayr Observer" went on sale in 1832. Among its editors were Ferguson, Provost of Ayr 1888-91, and James Paterson, author of a noted history of Ayrshire. This photograph shows the workers at the printworks in Union Arcade in 1897. Back left to right: R Wight, Geary, W Hannah, A Muir, Greenlees, Ferguson, Noble, A Muir, W Morrison, J Murray, Gildea, T Morrison, J Muir, Campbell, A Logan, Reid, Begg, Millar, J Wight, MacDonald, W Rowan, anon., J Sweeney, F Dickson, J Vallance. Front: Dobson, W Vallance, MacCutcheon, Nickelson, Mitchell. The "Observer" ceased production in 1930.

THE SEA FRONT—This aerial photograph of the sea front of Ayr shows many of the town's significant landmarks. In the centre are the County Buildings, facing the gardens with the Steven Fountain at their centre. At the opposite side of the buildings is Wellington Square with its cenotaph. To the right of the gardens is the Pavilion sitting on the Low Green. The bowling green in Bath Place can be seen, and in the foreground the houses of Queen's Terrace. The large house in the top right corner was known as Glendoon House but today is the Fairfield House Hotel.

LOW GREEN AND BANDSTAND—The band stand which formerly stood on the Low Green was erected in the Victorian era. The Green has been a place of enjoyment for the citizens of the town as well as to tourists for many years, and this scene shows a number of people enjoying the summer weather earlier this century. The large houses behind are, from right to left, Glendoon, Alloway Park and Park Terrace. The bandstand was removed during the winter of 1951-52, when a new shelter was created on the Esplanade.

THE ACADEMY—This early photograph is of one of the classrooms in the Academy. It shows a typical scene of the period, with children arranged in rows. Taken around 1900, the pupils are being taught by Lawrence Anderson who was the Writing Master, but who was noted for his work in developing art classes. Known as "Pluto" by the children, Anderson was renowned for preferring the cane to the tawse, but was recognised for being able to get the children to produce top quality work. Anderson taught at the Academy from 1858 until 1902, dying in 1923 at the age of ninety. The lower photograph, taken from the Academy Magazine of 1954, shows the prefects. Back left to right: A.M. Pollock, A. Jamieson, G.R. Sleight, G. Robertson, I. Drummond, R. MacNay, R. Alexander, T.M. Gilchrist, W. Hastie, E. Barr, A.S. MacClymont. Middle: A. Johnson, M. Anderson, E. Weir, M. Carmichael, B. Leask, M. Mair, C. Bryden, F. Smith, A. Graham, H. Ramage, M. Kay, J. Russell. Front: S. Scott, P. Cutt, L. Smith, S. Pollock, Mr J.Douglas Cairns (Rector 1945-65), Miss Marion MacWilliam (Woman Adviser 1946-62), J. Connolly, W. Inglis, P. Connolly, H. Crawford.

ACADEMY RUGBY XV - Taken in 1958 , this was the rugby team of that season. Back - D. Caskie, D Taylor, J. Houston, J. F. Ure, J. MacCloy, J. Anderson, D. Stobie, D. Wardrop, T. Maxwell, Middle - J. Gunn, R. Bryden, J. D. Cairns (Rector), J. Hay, T. Watson (Gamesmaster), M. Denness, D. Duncanson, Front - I. MacLauchlan, J. Craig, and S. Kerr. Michael Denness later became noted as the captain of the England Cricket Squad, making over 25,000 runs in his first class career and hitting four test centuries. Ian "Mighty Mouse" MacLauchlan played Rugby 43 times for his country, captaining Scotland 19 times. J.F. (Ian) Ure was capped 11 times for football, playing for Dundee and Arsenal.

THE BIG STAMPWORKS—Known locally as the "Big Stampworks", the proper name of this factory is the Neptune Works. The factory dates from 1900 and was extended during the second war. At one time it had Britain's largest drop forge hammer, the sound of which disturbed residents in the locality for years. The works have made a variety of heavy engineering goods over the years, from lorry crankshafts and beams to components for the North Sea Oil industry. Operated by Scottish Stampings, the company was taken over by the G.K.N. group in 1953 and the United Engineering Steels Group in March 1986.

FOREHILL KIRK HOUSE—Forehill Farm, which had been bought by the town council, was in September 1952 leased by the Auld Kirk. Here the Kirk House was established, with a church created within a former barn. As the housing scheme of Forehill was extended, it was decided to set up a charge on 10th October 1956, with Revd. David Munro inducted as minister. The kirk in the barn continued to operate until Castlehill Parish Church was opened in 1958. The farm was subsequently demolished and the Church of Jesus Christ of Latter Day Saints was erected in its place.

ST COLUMBA'S PARISH CHURCH—Originally known as the Trinity Church, St Columba's was dedicated on 2nd October 1902. It was built of red sandstone to the plans of John Bennie Wilson of Glasgow. The hall had been erected in 1898. The organ was inaugurated on 26th January 1904 and the manse purchased in 1921. The church has a chime of eight bells by Harrington of Coventry, first rung in September 1905. The church contains stained glass by Sydney Holmes and C.C. Baillie, one memorial window commemorating Richard C. MacLaurin. In 1988 the church had the largest congregation in Ayr, with almost 1800 members.

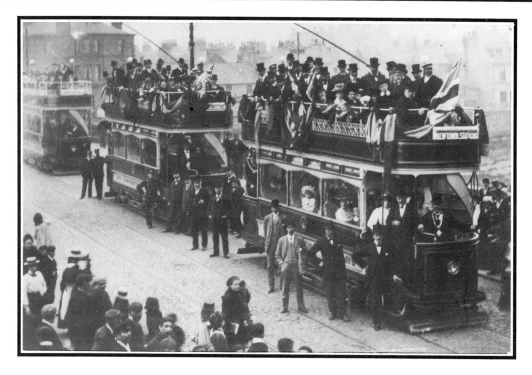

AYR BURGH TRAMWAYS—From 1901 until 1931 tramcars were a common sight passing through the streets of Ayr. The upper picture was taken on the official opening day, 26th September 1901, and shows a procession of trams crossing the New Bridge, the council having five at that time. The tramlines, which had a gauge of 4 feet 8½ inches, extended from Prestwick Cross down Main Street, along the High Street and thence out to St Leonards, a distance of four miles. A double track was permitted by an act of 1904 and this was laid on the stretch from near the depot to the junction of Midton and Carrick roads. At first tall poles were placed in the centre of the roads to support the power cable, but these were later replaced with wall brackets mounted on adjacent buildings. On the single-track stretches a total of thirteen passing loops were made. An extension was made to Alloway and opened on 1st June 1902 and to Hawkhill via George Street in 1908 in order to serve the new racecourse. The tram depot was located in Prestwick Road, seen in the lower photograph. The last tram ran on 31st December 1931. The tram company was bought over by Western S.M.T. in 1932 who disposed of the trams and replaced the service with buses.

AYR FORT FOOTBALL CLUB—Taken in 1905, this photograph shows the Ayr Fort football team which won the Ayr Juvenile League and Ayrshire Post Silver Ball that season. The team comprised of: Back: J.B. Fraser, A.M. MacLeod, J.L. Hutcheon, P.J. Boyle, A. Stewart. Middle: W. Fergusson (Vice President), A.A. Fraser, H. Rowan, H.S. MacNair, J.A. Campbell, J. Goodwin, J. Sinclair (President). Front: G. Bone, J.L. Goodwin.

HEATHFIELD HOSPITAL—It took an interlocutor by the Court of Session to compel the Burgh of Ayr to build a hospital for treating infectious diseases, the only such case in Scotland resulting from the Public Health Act of 1897. The burgh bought 12 acres at Heathfield in 1897 and there built Heathfield Hospital, formally opened on 30th June 1905. It had cost £21,000 to build. The hospital had various detached buildings for treating scarlet fever, enteric fever, diptheria, cholera and erysipelas. Extensions were added in 1937 and 1962. The hospital was sold for redevelopment in 1992.

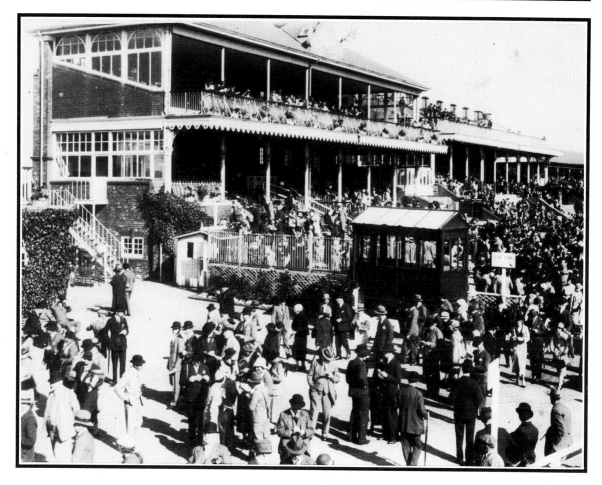

NEW RACECOURSE—The new racecourse off Whitletts Road was established in 1907, replacing the old racecourse on the south side of the town. The financing and management of the course was undertaken by the Western Meeting Club. The local architect Allan Stevenson designed the complex, in association with the Newmarket architects, W.C. and A.S. Manning. Regular races are held throughout the year, notably the Scottish Grand National in March and Ayr Gold Cup in September. The Eglinton Rooms were erected in 1967, to the plans of J. and J.A. Carrick. Within the racecourse complex is a statue of the famous horse, "Red Rum", sculpted by Annette Yarrow in 1975. The upper photograph shows the crowds gathering for the Gold Cup in 1933, the lower picture of the horses and jockeys shortly after the gates had opened with Dalmilling farm behind. The stand shown in the upper picture replaced the one which was on 4th April 1913 set on fire by the sufragettes following the arrest of Emily Pankhurst. The stand had cost £3000 to erect, having a luncheon room and Stewards' Room within.

WHYTOCK'S CLOSE—There used to be many closes and back lanes in Ayr and Newton, but redevelopment has obliterated many of these. This photograph shows Whytock's Close which was quite typical of most. A pend leads through the buildings of Main Street, which could allow a cart pulled by horses through, and small buildings and places of business line the alleyway. The close got its name from Whytock's Buildings, owned by James Whytock, which was located at 7 Main Street. At that time run as a smithy, the back yard was later developed as a garage, and is now occupied by the MFI showroom.

POLLOCK'S LEMONADE FACTORY—Pollocks's aerated water company was founded in 1840, originally having its works and bottling plant at 18 River Street, formerly part of the Black Bull. Peter Pollock established a new aerated water factory in Sym's Lane off Limond's Wynd in 1908. The factory was designed by William Cowie and occupied the site of the original "Wooden Kirk". The factory produced lemonade and had its own bottling plant. The drawing shows the new factory with, on the extreme right, the replacement Wooden Kirk. The site of the factory is currently a car park at Kings Court.

WALLACETOWN SCHOOL FOOTBALL CLUB—Wallacetown School had a reputation for training good footballers. This photograph was taken in 1909 when the team were the schools champions for that season. The school was erected at the end of Church Street in 1875 to replace a smaller building in King Street. An extension was added to the school in 1935. In 1952 the school was converted to a nursery school and in 1992 had 240 children taught by sixteen staff.

WHITLETTS PRIMARY SCHOOL—The school at Whitletts was erected in 1909-10 to replace an older and smaller building. The architect was A.C. Thomson. In 1988 the school had approximately 150 pupils on the roll.

SIR JAMES FERGUSSON'S STATUE—Sir James Fergusson was born in Edinburgh in 1832, son of Sir Charles Fergusson of Kilkerran. He was elected to Parliament for Ayrshire in 1854 and Manchester N.E. in 1885. He was appointed Governor of South Australia (1868-73), New Zealand (1873-5) and Bombay (1880-85). He was also Under Secretary of State for Foreign Affairs, for India, and at the Home Office, and Postmaster General for a time. Fergusson was killed by an earthquake in Kingston, Jamaica, in January 1907. The statue was sculpted by Sir Goscombe John and unveiled in October 1910 by the Earl of Eglinton.

SOUTH AYRSHIRE LIBERAL CLUB—Located at the corner of the Sandgate and Boswell Park, Ayr and South Ayrshire Liberal Club was erected in 1911 at a cost of £5000. The architect was J.R. Johnstone of Troon. The building had two shops on the ground floor, a smoking, ladies and reading room on the first. The second floor had a billiard room with two tables and a caretaker's flat. At the time of opening, on 27th July, the secretary of the club was W.H. MacCosh, solicitor, Wellington Chambers.

MILLAR'S BUILDINGS—In 1896 Thomas Millar, provision merchant, developed the corner of Cross Street and Limond's Wynd with the erection of 44 homes. These had from one to three apartments, and there was a water-closet for every two homes. A new feature for Ayr at the time was the inclusion of an ash-chute. The architect was H.V. Eaglesham and they cost £8000 to build. Three business premises were located on the ground floor, the corner site occupied by the Wallacetown Bar. At the back of the sketch is Russell Street School. The "Prince of Wales" bar now occupies the site of Millar's Buildings.

THE PAVILION—Erected by the town council to the plans of James Kennedy Hunter of Ayr, the Pavilion is still a major centre for entertainment, opening on 25th May 1911. Dancing, concerts and roller skating have been held in it from that time to the present. The Popplewell family operated it from 1913 until 1967, excluding 1918-22. The style of the building is unusual, with four tall towers, and the balusters at the front entrance came from the original New Bridge. The council put the building up for sale in 1992, but changed its mind and Christine Ridha managed to retain her lease.

NEWTON ACADEMY—This school was erected in 1911 to the plans of William Cowie. An earlier building had previously occupied the same site, erected in 1847 by the Burgh of Newton. The school later became a junior secondary school and latterly a primary school until it was closed in 1970. It acted for a time as the Technical Annexe of Ayr Academy, but was converted into a teachers' resource centre and base for education advisers.

SEAFIELD CHILDREN'S HOSPITAL—Originally the home of Sir William Arrol, Seafield House was in 1921 acquired by Ayrshire Health Authority as a maternity and child welfare hospital. It had previously acted as an auxiliary hospital during the Great War. The house cost £16,500 and alterations and furnishings another £3,500. From 1947 nurses were trained here and an extension was added in 1952. In 1944 the hospital was converted to a paediatric unit only, and served as such until 1991. It is now the health board's headquarters. The film "No Time for Tears" starring Anna Neagle was filmed at the hospital.

THE WEE STAMPWORKS—Properly known as the Victoria Stamping Works of James Dickie and Company, the "Wee Stampworks" produce steel and iron castings and forgings. At first the company produced parts for ships, steam engines and industrial equipment, but today components are made for the automotive, defence, mining and oil industries. The company was founded in 1913 at the newly-erected works in Somerset Road. The lower photograph shows the works that year, with the Newton Park School in the centre, the big stampworks to the right and the Hawkhill Chemical Works behind Dickie's. The photograph was taken from Lochside Road over the fields where Wilson Street is now. An extension to the works with a new foundry was added in 1953. A further extension known as the Heathfield Foundry was created at Seaforth Road. The company employed 140 people in 1974. In January 1992 the employees bought the company from the Dickie family who had remained in control until that time. Today the company employs around 85 people and continues to produce drop forgings up to ninety pounds in weight.

THE BUS STATION—In 1924 ground off Fullarton Street was redeveloped as a bus station, where from 1932 SMT buses had their Ayr terminus. Seven platforms were used for different destinations. This view was taken looking towards Douglas Street, with the rear of Green's Playhouse visible. Note in the photograph the hand cart used for transporting parcels and luggage. The stance was rebuilt in 1978. A second bus station was located on the opposite side of Boswell Park at the corner with Arthur Street, established by A.A. Motor Services in 1931.

HANNAH DAIRY RESEARCH INSTITUTE—The institute was established in 1928 and named after John Hannah of Girvanmains. The building was designed by A.G.Ingham and erected in 1931. Here various tests and experiments are carried out to further the dairy industry, in association with the Agricultural and Food Research Council. Cattle, sheep and goats are kept. There are approximately two hundred members of staff. In a small garden area is a bronze sculpture entitled "The Milkmaid". This was the work of Denys Mitchell, a blacksmith from Kelso, who created the figures from welded sheet steel.

COUNTY BUILDINGS—The new County Buildings were added on to the Court House from 1931-35, the architect being Alex Mair. The foundation stone was laid by the Duke of York (later King George VI) on 10th July 1931. He was accompanied by his wife Elizabeth now the Queen Mother. Built round a courtyard, the buildings were erected on the site of the old gaol. Below ground level cellars were constructed to act as air raid shelters in the event of war. The west facade is adorned with the arms of Ayr County Council and the motto "God Schaw the Richt", matriculated in 1890 and 1931.

SANDGATE FIRE STATION—The Fire Station at 13 Sandgate was opened in 1930, at a cost of £8074, designed by T. O'Beirne. This picture shows the firemen around that time. Back left to right: T Dunn, F Hastings, P Tierney, Ross, P Duncan, M Ivory. Middle: A MacEwen, H Dunn, T Ivory, J Morrison, J Cooper, J Neil, I MacGregor, A Dalton, T Bruce. Front: Deputy Convenor Bowie, Firemaster Galloway, T Murray and Provost James Gould. Previously the station was located in the close behind the house. The first motorised fire engine had been purchased in 1914, followed by others in 1921 and 1927.

HEATHFIELD SCHOOL—Opened in 1931, the school at Heathfield was built as a result of an increasing population in the district and because of overcrowding in other nearby schools. In 1928 it was noted that there had been 554 houses erected at or near the Prestwick boundary. The ground was acquired in 1929 and J.S. Williamson prepared plans for the building, initially designed to cope with 400 pupils. The cost of building the school was estimated at £14,435, the contractors including Henderson of Prestwick and Inglis of Kilmarnock. This sketch was prepared by the architect.

ORIENT PICTURE HOUSE—The Orient Picture House was built in Main Street, opposite the Newton Steeple, in 1932. The plans were drawn up by Albert V. Gardner who produced a unique interior in an Oriental or Moorish style. This has been changed in recent years. Externally a centrally-placed turret is a unique feature. The building has since been converted to a bingo hall and social club.

VISIT OF SIR HARRY LAUDER—Harry Lauder, the famous Scots comedian and entertainer, visited Newton Manse on 1st July 1933 to open a Garden Fete. He is seen here in his kilt, with the Revd. P.L.K. Mudie by his side. In his speech, Lauder said: "A friend met me this morning and asked me where I was off to. 'Newton upon Ayr,' said I. 'Where's that?' he asked. (Laughter from the audience) 'It's the best bit of Ayr,' said I. (Laughter) I don't know whether it is or not! (Laughter) But it's the best bit of Ayr the day that I am here!'

ROYAL BURGH COUNCIL—Taken on 6th May 1935, this group photograph shows the councillors and officials of the Royal Burgh. They were, back: Hugh Wright, Robert Lyle, James Dunlop, George MacDowall, Dr James Grant, William Steen. Middle: Peter Smith, William MacDowall, John Richardson, Adam Hart, John Young, James Lowdon, P.A. Thomson, James Smith, William Alexander, James Currie, T.L. Robb, Robert Paterson, William Miller. Front: William Ross, John Stewart, Robert Bowman, Hugh Mackie, Thomas Murray, Provost Thomas Galloway, James Wills, William MacLean, Peter Boyle and Thomas Wilson.

GAIETY THEATRE—The Gaiety Theatre in Carrick Street was erected in 1902 but was damaged by fire and had to be rebuilt the following year. The photograph on the left shows the interior of the theatre as it was prior to a second fire which took place on 2nd August 1955. There was a possibility that the theatre would have closed at that time, but a campaign by audiences and artistes alike resulted in its total refurbishment. The lower photograph shows a "Gaiety Whirl" of 1952 with the well-known comedian Aly Wilson.

ICE RINK—Ayr Ice Rink was erected in Beresford Terrace in 1939 to the plans of James Carrick. It promoted the sports of skating, ice hockey and curling. Ice hockey was played by the Ayr Raiders and the juvenile Ayr Spitfires. A new ice rink was built in Limekiln Road on the site of an old greyhound racing stadium and opened in 1974.

THE HOME GUARD—During the second World War (in May 1940) Local Defence Volunteers were organised to provide the first form of attack in case of German invasion. These were soon known as the Home Guard, or "Dad's Army" in fun. The Ayr guard (7th Ayrshire battalion) organised road blocks, air raid shelters and took part in a camp at Croy Bay. This photograph shows the members of Ayr Home Guard at that time. As the war came to a close it was realised that the Home Guard were no longer required. The official "Stand Down" parade took place in December 1944.

BUTLINS HOLIDAY CAMP—Butlins Holiday Camp at the Heads of Ayr was opened in 1947. Previously the camp had been known as H.M.S. Scotia, a naval base created in 1941. Trains brought hundreds of holidaymakers to the complex, reached from the Heads of Ayr Station by cablecar. It had chalets, pools, trains, boats, shows, and a church. The site underwent various rebuildings and extensions to create Wonderwest in 1988, attracting 100,000 residents in its first season, with a further 190,000 people enjoying day visits. This old postcard shows the "Sunshine Chalets" while below we have "Wondersplash" a modern indoor water complex complete with rapid river and flumes.

GRAMMAR SCHOOL—The Grammar School in Midton Road was erected in 1868 at a cost of £1,300, subscribed for by the sale of shares at £1 each. The fees were around half those charged by the Academy, and the school soon gained its place as the middle school for the burgh. In 1899 there were around 400 pupils on the roll. The building was rebuilt and extended in 1909. The school became a junior secondary in 1947, but in 1973 was lowered to a primary school. This class photograph dates from sometime in the 1950s.

CIVIC THEATRE—The town council purchased the former Robertson Memorial Church and converted it to a theatre, John Dickie providing the plans. The theatre was opened on 16th April 1951 by the actor Duncan McCrae. The stage is just 22 feet by 16 feet, and the auditorium can seat 352 theatre-goers. The first performance staged in 1954, was "Arms and the Man" by George Bernard Shaw. The Civic was the first theatre of its kind in Scotland, and it still caters principally for amateur theatrical shows, ballets, marionette and professional repertory company productions.

CATHEDRAL OF THE GOOD SHEPHERD—The Roman Catholic place of worship in Dalmilling Crescent was in 1961 granted cathedral status, being designated the seat of the Bishop of Galloway. By tradition, having a cathedral makes a town a city, and some have claimed such for Ayr. The chapel was designed by John Torry and erected 1955-7, being opened in September 1957 by Gordon Gray, Archbishop of St Andrews. The cost of construction was £64,000. It underwent refurbishment in 1985, using fittings from St Robert's Chapel in Bellarmine, and stained glass from St Margaret's in Kinning Park, both Glasgow.

ROYAL SCOTS FUSILIERS WAR MEMORIAL—Located in a small garden next to the County Buildings is the Royal Scots Fusiliers war memorial. The bronze statue was sculpted by Pilkington Jackson in 1960 and bears the inscription: *THIS STATUE WAS RAISED BY THEIR COMRADES IN PROUD AND GRATEFUL MEMORY OF THOSE ROYAL SCOTS FUSILIERS WHO GAVE THEIR LIVES IN THE WORLD WAR 1939-1945. THEY DIED THAT WE MIGHT REMAIN FREE.* The granite wall behind commemorates the services of the RSF from its formation in 1678 until its partnership with the Highland Light Infantry in 1959 to form the Royal Highland Fusiliers.

NEW FIRE STATION—The present fire station is located at the junction of John Street and Station Road, previously the site of Content House. It was erected in 1963, the tall tower used for both practising and for the drying of hosepipes. Stone from Content House was used in the construction of some of the walls. The architects of the fire station were J & JA Carrick. The South Western Area Fire Brigade, which covered the four counties of south-west Scotland, was instituted in 1948.

FIRE FIGHTING — The South Western Area Headquarters and Fire Station was opened on 10th May 1963 jointly by Daniel Sim, Convenor of Ayr County Council, and William Cowan, Provost of Ayr. Built on the site of Content House, the station replaced the old one in the Sandgate. The photograph shows firemen at work tackling a blaze in the High Street on the 29th June 1977. An electrical fault in the basement of Greenlees' shop caused a fire which spread into neighbouring cellars and up into "Tramps".

CRAIGIE COLLEGE OF EDUCATION—Established in 1964 as a teacher training college, the buildings were erected in the grounds of Craigie House. Courses in primary, early and nursery education are offered, as well as social care. The architect of the main building was Buchanan Campbell, the halls of residence, with sixty rooms, added in 1967 by Boswell Mitchell & Johnston, a further thirty-five rooms provided in 1974. The music and drama departments are located in Craigie House. Craigie College became Paisley University's Faculty of Education following threats of closure. These students graduated in 1984.

TECHNICAL COLLEGE—Ayr Technical College was erected off Content Avenue in 1966 to the plans of Charles Toner. The college replaced the former technical school which was located at St Leonard's School. The name has in recent years been shortened to Ayr College. A new library costing £150,000 was opened within the college in 1993 by Robert Campbell, chairman of the College Council.

MAINHOLM ACADEMY—Mainholm High School opened for its first term in 1965. It became an academy in 1968. The adjoining building, which had been erected as Queen Margaret Academy in 1966, was in 1975 incorporated into Mainholm, creating North and South schools with a capacity for 1800 pupils. In 1988 there were less than 700 in attendance, however. The excess space was partially used by the former St Catherine's Primary School which was closed, the new school now being called the Good Shepherd School.

THE CAIRN—Located in Cairn Crescent, Alloway, this memorial stands on the site of the prehistoric cairn which Tam o' Shanter passed on his epic canter to the Auld Brig o' Doon. According to the poem this is where "hunters fand the murder'd bairn." The cairn, which stands about four feet tall, has a bronze plaque inscribed: *'And through the whins and by the cairn.' To perpetuate that eventful journey of 'Tam' to Alloway Kirk, this cairn was re-erected through the co-operation of Ayr Town Council, the Burns Federation and John Dickie & Son, Ltd. Builders, July 1965.*

MASONHILL CREMATORIUM—The crematorium at Masonhill was opened on 11th July 1966 by Andrew Kerr JP, Chairman of the Heath Board of Ayr County Council. Designed by the county architects, Douglas Hay under Clarke Fyfe, the crematorium was intended to serve most of the county. In 1971 the crematorium dealt with 1227 cremations, 28% of the county's deaths. Within the simply-finished chapel are softwood beams and roof panels. The building has a slate roof, fyfestone and harl walls and cast concrete porticos. A small garden of remembrance and ponds are located outside.

ST PAUL'S R.C. CHURCH—The Roman Catholic church of St Paul in Peggieshill Road at Belmont was erected between 1964, when the plans were passed, and 1967, when the church was opened. Proposals for a new Catholic place of worship for the south side of the town had been mooted since 1956. The chapel, presbytery and garage cost around £40,000 to construct. A large modern building, in 1988 it had 1,600 members.

PRESTWICK CIRCUITS—Founded in 1969 in a small building at a former colliery at Prestwick, Prestwick Circuits established a new 20,000 square feet factory at Mosshill Industrial Estate in 1973 to make printed circuit boards for the computer and electronics industry. This has since expanded to over four times the size and a second factory was opened at Irvine in 1983. In that year there were 240 employees at Mosshill and the company is one of western Europe's largest manufacturers of printed circuits.

DIGITAL EQUIPMENT FACTORY—This aerial photograph of Mosshill Industrial Estate shows the factory of Digital Equipment (Scotland) Limited. Digital opened a pilot plant of 25,000 square feet here in 1976 which quickly extended to over 400,000 square feet, and currently employing over 1200 people. Originally involved in final assembly and test systems, the Ayr factory was responsible for designing and manufacturing the MicroVAX 3100 computer. On the extreme right of the photograph is the factory of Prestwick Circuits.

KIRKING OF THE COUNCIL—The town council of Ayr were traditionally "kirked" each year after the November election, but following the local government reorganisations of 1975 the tradition has died. The last "kirking" took place in 1974, when the councillors marched from the chambers to the Auld Kirk, led by pipers. This photograph shows them returning via the Fish Cross, with a halberdier leading, followed by the mace carrier and Provost Campbell Howie. The council met for the last time on 15th May 1975 before Kyle and Carrick District Council took over.

KYLE ACADEMY—Erected on the lands of Holmston, Kyle Academy was built to serve the growing suburbs east of the town, as well as the nearby village of Coylton. The school opened in August 1979 and gained full six year status in 1984. Built to accomodate 800 pupils, the roll in 1991 was 768.

WEST SOUND RADIO—West Sound, operated by Radio Ayrshire Ltd, started broadcasting on 15th October 1980. On 21st May 1990 broadcasts commenced from a second studio in Dumfries, known as South West Sound. In 1985 the company diversified into running nursing homes. The radio station organises the largest Burns Supper in the world. Held in Glasgow each year the Burns Supper raises money for charity from paying guests and phone in contributors. The photograph shows Joe Campbell and staff of West Sound Radio outside the recently extended Radio House in Holmston Road.

AYR UNITED FOOTBALL CLUB—United was formed in April 1910 when Ayr Parkhouse and Ayr F.C. merged. Ayr F.C.'s ground at Somerset was kept as the home park, and the team's first game (against Port Glasgow) was a two-nil victory. This photograph was taken in 1992 and shows, back left to right: Barry Scott, Nigel Howard, Cammy Duncan, Ally Graham, Michael Robertson, Ally Fraser, Eddie O'Donnell. Middle: Greig Hood, John Traynor, Willie Farthy, Gary Agnew, Paul MacLean, Tommy Walker, Gordon Mair, Derek Allan. Front: Ian Cardle, Lauchlan Millar, Duncan George, David Kennedy, George Burley, Alan MacTurk, Lee Gardiner, Cortez Clark, Dale Roberts.

MILL STREET—Taken in 1986, this photograph shows the old tannery prior to its demolition, with what was Templeton's carpet factory behind. The tannery was operated by Harry Beebee and previously by R. Dobbie & Company. The louvred upper flats allowed the drying of hides. The tannery was closed in 1979, having been taken over by the Bridge of Weir Leather Company. The building to the left of the tannery (with the arched windows) was Thomas Murray's ice factory. The street has basically been rebuilt with blocks of flatted houses, including Mill Wynd, Blackfriars Walk and Kirk Care's sheltered housing.

GATEWAY SUPERSTORE—A number of old buildings between Wallace Street and Garden Street were demolished to make way for the new Gateway superstore, erected in 1986-87 to plans by Cowie, Torry and Partners. During the excavations green glazed pottery dating from the 1300s was found as well as the original cobbled yard of the Black Bull Inn. This view, taken in May 1986, is of work underway on the construction of the shop, a steel frame being erected prior to brick infill and glazing being added. The shop has since been taken over by Asda.

THE AYR HOSPITAL—The new Ayr Hospital was opened in 1991 to replace the older hospitals of Heathfield, Seafield and Ayr County. Built on a greenfield site behind the Ailsa Hospital, the architects were Keppie Henderson of Glasgow. In 1993 the building was extended to provide a new Day Surgery Unit and Patients' Hotel. A helicopter pad was provided, and there were proposals to create a rail link. The hospital deals with around 2500 accident and emergency patients every month, with a further 10,000 appointments at the out-patients clinic.

CARRICK GLEN HOSPITAL—Built on the Dalmellington Road at Glenparks farm, the Carrick Glen Hospital is operated by the Independent British Hospital Association. Built in 1991-92, the architects were the Elliott Manning Partnership. The hospital has twenty-two beds and offers a range of surgical, diagnostic and out-patient facilities.

FLOWER SHOW —The first flower show took place in the Dam Park Hall in 1960, organised by the Director of Parks and Recreation, Robert Wakefield. The first show was comparatively small, but by 1983 it had grown to become Scotland's biggest flower show attracting thirty thousand visitors. Indeed, it outgrew the hall and has been relocated to Rozelle Park, where a number of huge marquees are erected to house the thousands of exhibits. These include the large municipal entries down to children's model gardens. Also on show are various handicrafts including shepherds crooks, the photograph being of David Raeside, winner in 1993.

AGRICULTURAL SHOW —Ayr show is organised by the Ayrshire Agricultural Association (founded 1835) and the first event took place in 1852, held in Beresford Park. In 1897 it moved to the Dam Park (which the association had bought) before moving on to the new racecourse in 1946 where it continues to be held. One of Scotland's premier agricultural shows, farmers and others from all over the south-west flock to the show to exhibit their finest stock, or else just to browse amongst the trade stands. The photograph shows Murray Stevenson with his prizewinning Ayrshire cow. "Bankend Lady Luck 11th" in 1985.

BORDERLINE THEATRE COMPANY —Formed in 1974 to bring theatre to the community, the Borderline Theatre Group performed to just five thousand people in its first year of existence. The company has grown since then, performing to more than 37,000 people in 1994. In 1986 the Darlington Church in North Harbour Street was acquired by them and has since been converted to a small theatre and practise centre. The group like to produce an alternative pantomime each year, and tour the county taking performances into the Community. The photograph above shows the Borderline Theatre Group cast of "A Call to Arms" while below Craig Ferguson and Gerard Kelly are photographed in a scene from the 1994 production of "The Odd Couple".

SYDNEY DEVINE —One of the most noted of Ayr's recent residents is the singer Sydney Devine. Born in Cleland in Lanarkshire, he left school and went to London where he played the juvenile lead in the musical "Wild Grows the Heather". He is noted for country singing and has sold many albums and singles, his first LP appearing in 1970. His biggest hit was "Scotland Forever" in 1978. After illness he retired from singing in the late 1980s. He continued in the entertainment business, however, as mine host of the Annfield Hotel and as a presenter on West Sound Radio. Sydney also performed many times in pantomime at the Gaiety and elsewhere.

ALLY McLEOD —In football circles one of Ayr's most celebrated residents is Ally McLeod. He was born in Glasgow in 1931 and played football for Third Lanark, St Mirren, Blackburn, Hibs and Ayr. He became manager of Ayr United from 1966 until 1975 when he moved to take on the same job at Aberdeen. It was during his spell at Aberdeen that he was selected to become the manager of the Scottish World Cup squad which played in Argentina in 1978. He returned as manager of Ayr for a spell in 1978, moved to Motherwell then Airdrie and returned to Ayr 1985-90. The photograph shows him with the silver salver which he won as Ayr's citizen of the year in 1972.

CREE LODGE STABLES —The stables at Cree Lodge have been in existence for over one hundred years. Many winning horses and jockeys have come from the lodge and trainers include Mr McGuigan, Mr Wightman, Nigel Angus, Charlie Williams and John Wilson. The present, and first lady trainer is Linda Perratt who has been there since 1991. She does both National Hunt and Flat training and has produced over fifty winners in three years, including wins at Epsom with Petite D'argent, ridden by Ray Cochrane and owned by Danny Cupar and George Hosie, a horse which cost only 680 guineas, and at Aintree with Persuasive. The stables can accommodate up to 36 horses.